Life
Below Stairs

he Real Lives of Servants, 1939 to the Present

PAMELA HORN

AMBERLEY

This edition first published 2014

Amberley Publishing
The Hill, Stroud
Gloucestershire, GL5 4EP

www.amberley-books.com

British Library Cataloguing in Publication Data.
A catalogue record for this book is available from the British Library.

ISBN 978-1-4456-1898-2 (paperback)
ISBN 978-1-4456-1910-1 (ebook)

Typesetting and Origination by Amberley Publishing.
Printed in Great Britain.

CONTENTS

Shillings and Pence Conversion Table

Old Money	Decimal	Old Money	Decimal
1d	½p	1s 8d	8½p
2d or 3d	1p	1s 9d or 10d	9p
4d	1½p	1s 11d	9½p
5d	2p	2s	10p
6d	2½p	2s 6d	12½p
1s	5p	3s	15p
1s 1d	5½p	5s	25p
1s 2d or 1s 3d	6p	10s	50p
1s 6d	7½p	20s	100p, i.e £1

PREFACE

The twentieth century saw a transformation in the scale and nature of paid household employment. At the beginning of the century domestic service was still the largest single, female occupation, as it had been during the reign of Queen Victoria. For vast numbers of middle- and upper-class householders, the employment of resident servants was an accepted part of family life. Although recruitment problems were already emerging before 1914, it was the First World War which witnessed the first real changes in that well-established pattern, as many domestics seized the opportunity to pursue other careers.

High unemployment in the 1920s and 1930s forced numerous women, in particular, to make a reluctant return to household work, but the seeds of a new order had already been sown. Recruitment drives were undertaken and government training programmes were provided, while female refugees fleeing persecution in Nazi Germany found, often enough, that their only hope of entering Britain was to become a maid. But despite these efforts, domestic labour was never again to be freely available in the way it had been in the nineteenth century.

After the Second World War this was even more clearly apparent. State initiatives to boost domestic work, including the widening of the home help service, were again a feature of the years after 1945. However, overall the second half of the twentieth century saw a decline in the use of paid household labour. Only in the final decades of the century did that alter, as a new demand for cleaners and childcare providers arose from comfortably off, working couples and as older people living alone looked for help with household chores. Professional cleaning firms grew up to satisfy some part of this need. Also important were foreign domestic workers, particularly from the Philippines, Portugal and Spain. Their role was especially significant in the larger cities, including London.

The course of this process of change in domestic employment and the way it impinged upon the growth of the hotel and catering trades are discussed, as is the development of household service. Whereas once the recruitment of a maid was, at least in part, a status symbol as well as a useful adjunct to family life, by the 1990s the employment of a cleaner or a nanny was seen primarily in functional terms, to meet a particular need or to resolve a domestic problem. Only a comparatively few wealthy families still employed staff for reasons of prestige, rather than purely out of necessity. Even in these cases their requirements were often met by the recruitment of a married couple, with the husband acting as butler and his wife as cook-housekeeper. Additional workers were brought in on a daily basis to carry out cleaning duties or to provide extra help when important social functions were held.

The way in which this has affected the relationship between employer and worker is assessed. After all, domestic service is unlike any other occupation, as it involves bringing outsiders into the home where they may witness the intimacies of family life at close quarters including the tensions and the pleasures, the quarrels and the celebrations. Such a situation calls for a degree of discretion and diplomacy on the part of the worker to complement his or her skills in performing the household duties required, and respect from the employer for the feelings of the servant. That was as true at the end of the 1990s as it had been a century earlier, even if at both dates those high personal standards were not always met.

Part one

The Second World War and Beyond

The proportion of households that employed paid domestic help has never been large. . . . But among those who were accustomed to employ such help, the shortage and increasing cost of domestic labour have been keenly felt, particularly as conditions during and since the war have aggravated the difficulties of housekeeping. . . . The burden is felt in the actual domestic work, in the tie which children involve and in the physical and nervous strain of continuous care of children.

Report of the Royal Commission on Population, Cmd.
7695 (London, 1949), pp. 148-9.

THE PRESSURE OF WAR

Between 1939 and 1960 domestic service in Britain underwent a profound change both in its scale and its nature. In 1931 almost 5 per cent of households in England and Wales still employed a resident domestic; by 1951 that had fallen to about 1 per cent and in 1961 the figure was put at just 0.6 per cent.[1] Even if non-resident maids and those engaged in commercial establishments were included, the decline was sharp, with 1.3 million female servants recorded in England and Wales in 1931 and 0.72 million in 1951 – a fall of 46 per cent. Among the men, there was a reduction from just over 78,000 in 1931 to a little over 66,000 two decades later. Almost 41,000 of the latter were chefs, cooks and kitchen hands.[2] In Scotland, a similar picture emerged for women, with numbers falling from 138,679 in 1931 to 73,278 two decades later. For men, the situation differed slightly, as the 1931 figure of 4,543 had risen to 4,961 in 1951, but almost 4,000 of these were cooks, chefs and kitchen workers, mainly employed in commercial premises like hotels and restaurants. According to the census there were fewer than 1,000 'other' male domestic servants in Scotland in 1951.[3]

The Second World War played a major part in bringing about these developments, both psychologically and through its demands upon the nation's labour force. A contemporary report claimed that it had 'not so much solved as dissolved the whole structure of domestic service'.[4] Already before 1939 there had been a marked reluctance among women to take up paid domestic work and some of those who became servants were of indifferent quality. However, once female recruitment for industry and for the services got under way, the drift away from the occupation accelerated. A new spirit of egalitarianism made the thought of performing menial duties in private households unacceptable to many. Even those who continued with the work were often unenthusiastic. Thus a Kettering 'daily' confessed that while she was not ashamed of her employment, she much disliked continually meeting 'people who think of one as only the "char"; it doesn't add to one's self-respect by any means, particularly when some of those one works for, and is paid by, have less intelligence and consideration than oneself'.[5] Margaret Powell, who took up daily domestic work during the war to make ends meet, also resented the autocratic attitude of certain mistresses. One complained because Margaret failed to address her as 'Madam'.[6]

It was in these circumstances that the *Ministry of Labour Gazette* concluded that if household employment were 'to make its essential contribution to the health and welfare of the nation on the return of peace, a concerted and sustained effort would have to be made to eradicate the causes of its unpopularity'.[7] The effort was made, but the unpopularity persisted.

At the beginning of the war there was a general slowness to mobilise women, whereas for men conscription began immediately for those aged eighteen to forty-one (raised in December 1941 to an upper limit of fifty-one).[8] This affected traditional areas of male service, with gardeners (unless they could claim exemption as agricultural workers), gamekeepers and indoor domestics being called up or doing other war work.

The trend was reinforced by the widespread requisitioning of large country houses for military and other purposes.

Chatsworth was taken over by a girls' school and Woburn Abbey was used by the Imperial Intelligence Committee. Thousands of properties were commandeered, with the armed services requisitioning the majority of them for anything from barracks, billets, supply bases and officers' messes to strategic planning headquarters, or signals and training bases. The Air Ministry alone occupied twenty thousand properties and the Ministry of Health almost nineteen thousand.[9] This led to a reduced demand for domestic staff. In some cases, evacuees from the major industrial towns were dispersed to country houses and there they often encountered the hostility of the servants who looked after them. In September 1939 Violet Markham complained of 'snobbish and difficult' maids who 'when hostile to the incursion of strange children may create a very difficult problem for the mistress'.[10]

Evelyn Waugh's novel, *Put Out More Flags*, described the effect of evacuees on one fictional country house early in the war. On the morning after their arrival at Malfrey the head housemaid resigned, saying that with her bad legs she could not cope 'with children all over the place'. An hour later the three housemaids declared they were going to work in a factory. The butler and cook remained loyal, but the footman was due to leave for the army in a few weeks and the valet had already joined the yeomanry with his master. Out of doors the situation was little better. 'The leaves fell in the avenue at Malfrey, and this year, where once there had been a dozen men to sweep them, there were only four and two boys.'[11]

Many evacuees returned home after a few months, while in other cases cooks and housemaids came to accept the additional work the children created. *The Lady* praised the way most had considered it 'a patriotic service', to which they had risen 'nobly'.[12] In the summer of 1942, however, it became official policy to return as many evacuees as possible to their families so that the country houses they had occupied could be used by American troops preparing for D-Day.[13]

Much of the requisitioning proved long lasting and as a result buildings became dilapidated and even damaged, especially when used as barracks, while gardens were overgrown or were turned over to vegetable production. At Aynho, the army commandeered part of the mansion as well as large areas of the pleasure grounds and adjacent park. These became pockmarked with concrete emplacements, Nissen huts and petrol stores, while trees were felled and lawns neglected. In 1940 Ted Humphris, the head gardener, found himself tending the gardens virtually single-handed. In the summer of that year, at his employer's suggestion, he started running the greenhouses and the vegetable plot on his own account as a market garden and continued the arrangement for the duration of the war. This meant concentrating on food production, with house plants giving way to tomatoes in the greenhouses and luxuries like asparagus and strawberries being replaced by potatoes and other essential vegetables. Much produce was sold to villagers, although some customers came several miles from the market town of Banbury. The military also purchased produce. Initially, Ted's only help came from his wife and school-age son, plus a little casual assistance from neighbours on summer evenings. Not until the spring of 1941 did he secure the aid of a girl in her late teens with an interest in gardening. She provided much-needed energy and enthusiasm.[14]

Female participation in the war effort was part of a campaign promoted by the Women's Farm and Gardens Association whereby women aged between sixteen and forty were to be apprenticed to head gardeners for six months before taking on the duties of an under-gardener. The scheme was backed by the Ministry of Agriculture and the trainees had to demonstrate they were suitable for garden work and were unable to afford the fees of a horticultural college.[15] Within weeks the owners of forty large gardens had agreed to participate in the scheme, but the prediction that it would lead to a greater role for women gardeners after the war proved over-optimistic. In 1951 there were just 2,160 'other' female gardeners, that is not engaged in market gardening, in England and Wales, compared to 125,724 males so occupied. In Scotland, there were 206 women to 12,650 men.[16]

Feed restrictions leading to a prohibition on the artificial rearing of game birds and the shortage of gamekeepers and powder for cartridges brought a virtual end to game preservation, although, as at Elveden, periodic shoots continued to be held on some estates. In other places, there was a general emphasis on shooting for the pot.[17] At Eaton, the change was dramatic. When Norman Mursell returned after the war in February 1946, he found only four keepers, compared to twenty before the war.[18] Efforts were made to revive game preservation after 1945, but it was never on the pre-war scale.

Pheasant rearing was re-established in a major way in the early 1950s, when animal feed supplies improved, but the number of keepers remained low. In England and Wales, in 1951, there were 3,776 gamekeepers and game watchers whereas in 1931 there had been 10,706, a fall of almost two-thirds. In Scotland, the decline was rather less severe, with the 4,050 recorded in 1931 dropping to 2,126 twenty years later.[19] In the post-war world many estates still preserving game sought to exploit the financial possibilities by letting shoots to syndicates, as they had done before 1939, and also by arranging commercial shooting parties. That affected the kind of sport offered, since syndicates expected large bags. It meant a greater concentration on pheasants at the expense of partridges, whose yields were more variable. As one keeper, Angus Nudds, commented: 'You cannot expect a syndicate member to pay for a season's shooting only to be told he cannot shoot that year because the partridges have not been able to rear any young due to the wet summer.'[20]

Male indoor servants who enlisted often found military life easier than their civilian occupation. Arthur Inch, who joined the RAF in June 1940, considered it 'no hardship' after the long spells on duty to which he had been accustomed in service: 'In fact the comparatively shorter hours in the forces was a revelation to me, I'd never had so much free time plus all the free passes when going on leave.'[21] When the war ended, having enjoyed this greater liberty, he did not look for domestic employment, but became a silver cleaner for a firm of Edinburgh jewellers. Only in 1956, when he heard of an attractive vacancy for a butler through his brother, who had remained in service as a chauffeur, did he decide to return to domestic work.

Another former male servant, who had spent the first fourteen years of his working life as a footman, went into a factory during the war. He stayed there until he became redundant in the late 1960s. The employment exchange, 'learning of my previous experience in private service offered me a job in Buckingham Palace', but he turned it down. 'I had tasted freedom I had never known and all overtime paid.' He added: 'I have never regretted leaving private service.'[22]

During the war male staffs were much depleted as only older men or those who could gain exemption in some other way remained in domestic employment. At Cliveden, Edwin Lee and the housekeeper ran the household with a small core of co-workers, including a chef and some older married women who came in daily. To Rosina Harrison, Lady Astor's maid, however, the greatest change for long-established workers like herself was in their relationship with their employers. Under war pressures the distinctions between master and servant were blurred. 'We were family.' Rosina and Lord Astor's valet, Arthur, accompanied their employers on their travels, including to Plymouth, where Lady Astor was an MP and Lord Astor was Lord Mayor, and they experienced the severe bombing raids the city suffered at the time.[23]

Many junior female servants abandoned domestic work at an early stage. Among them was Phyllis Elms, who had reluctantly entered the kitchens of a large house in Wiltshire because her family considered it an appropriate occupation. Of her life in service, she declared bitterly: 'I loathed it. . . . Mostly because I think I had a lot of pride and . . . you have to bow and scrape to people, that's not on with me.'[24] When an ECKO factory was opened at Malmesbury, it took her two months to win her father's consent for her to work there, but eventually he relented. Her new job involved winding electrical coils for use in aeroplanes and in radar and wireless equipment. Not only did she earn more than in service (£1 2s 6d a week instead of £1 a month, plus board and lodging), but the hours were shorter and more regular and she had far more free time. She called the factory 'a gift from the gods'.[25]

Other women wanted to 'do their bit' because their menfolk were at the front or because they themselves wished to play an active role in the struggle. Frances Partridge's maid, Joan, announced she was taking up war work when her fiance was sent abroad. She got a job in an aeroplane factory[26] in the spring of 1941. However, in the early months of the war female participation was more limited. In official circles a view prevailed of what was appropriate for women, and only when serious labour shortages emerged did a different policy apply. Even then restrictions remained. Amy O'Connor, who left domestic service to become a signals operator in the ATS, felt she 'was helping England', but she would have liked to have used weapons – something from which women were barred. Years later, when expressing strong anti-Nazi sentiments, she added: 'They could have given me a gun and I would have gone. . . . There were quite a few of us asked, could we go out with the men? Could we take guns? They wouldn't let us.'[27]

All too often, indeed, as another female auxiliary drily observed, whatever women applied for, 'they . . . try to get one committed to working in a canteen'.[28] Eileen Balderson, who had wanted to take up transport duties, was rejected because she was too short, but when she told the WAAF authorities that she had been a domestic servant in civilian life, she was promptly made a batwoman.[29] Another former maid, Mary Mackenzie, became a WAAF waitress in a sergeants' mess and was plagued with sexual propositions from many of the groundcrew.[30]

Compulsory registration of both occupied and unoccupied females began for those aged nineteen to forty in March 1941 at local employment exchanges and by 1943 had been extended to those aged nineteen to fifty.[31] Women selected from the register were allocated jobs to which, if they refused to go, they could be 'directed' by law. Conscription of single women aged twenty to twenty-one began in January 1942 and mainly involved entry into the ATS or into munitions production, where labour shortages were greatest. By 1943 conscription had been extended to all single women aged nineteen to twenty-four. From February 1942, under the Employment of Women (Control of Engagement) Order females aged twenty to thirty (with certain exemptions) could be recruited only through employment exchanges, the aim being to ensure that they took work regarded as essential to the war effort. In January 1943 the Order was extended to those up to forty and at that time females could be directed into part-time as well as full-time posts. Throughout the war only single women were regarded as fully mobile and from September 1941 any unmarried female wishing to avoid conscription had to prove she had 'domestic responsibilities'.[32]

Servants were affected by this, particularly those in the age group covered by conscription. The historian of one Coventry firm mentioned a draft of girls from Brighton who had formerly worked in hotels, finding difficulty in adjusting to conditions in a drop-forging shop. They had never before heard any noise like the 'thunder of the great hammers'.[33]

Employers, meanwhile, were anxious to keep their maids and the issue was raised in parliament. In response to this pressure and to claims of personal hardship for the sick, the elderly and mothers with young children, the government accepted that 'essential domestic help' could be allowed.[34] There were demands, too, that 'hardship' households be supplied with servants by employment exchanges or through the home help service. By 1942 it had been agreed that in homes where there were expectant mothers, mothers with young children, sick and aged people or where the wife was engaged in war work as well as having domestic duties, the last remaining servant would not be called up.[35]

That did not solve the problem when maids left of their own accord and no replacement could be found. Farmers' wives, too, complained of the added pressure of catering for extra workers at harvest and at other busy seasons along with their normal agricultural and domestic responsibilities. In February 1943 a Wiltshire farmer's wife described how she was being asked to provide either food and lodgings for additional members of the Women's Land Army or accommodation for Italian prisoners-of-war, as well as cooking for her own household of five, plus four Oxford undergraduates, who were helping and three single farm men who had to live in because of the shortage of cottages. She asked for a 'corps of women volunteers' to be raised to give 'even part-time help to farmhouses' during the 1943 harvest. 'The increasing load that is breaking down the farmers' wives will disrupt the organisation of the farms.'[36]

Many women, like Frances Partridge, reluctantly knuckled down to household chores, perhaps aided by a daily. In February 1944, Frances had Lawrence and Julia Gowing staying with her and noted that they were 'both heroic in the help they gave with bed-making and washing-up, and in Julia's case she hates it so much that it is heroism. When I said I didn't want any help with the cooking . . . she said "Ah yes, I understand and respect that", in a tone of great relief.'[37]

Such attitudes underlined the class differences identified in the Wartime Social Survey, with working-class contributors commenting sourly, 'people with money can do their bit towards the war by doing their own work and releasing maids'. Others did not see why 'women should go about with nothing to do, having a cook and a nannie. If a working man's wife can do work, they can!'[38]

A further cause of dissension was wealthy employers who continued to keep large staffs, thus evading the spirit of the regulations by recruiting servants above and below the registration ages, or else they employed married women, like Margaret Powell, with children under fourteen years, since they were exempt from regulation. In February 1941, *The Lady* condemned as a 'scandal' servant advertisements which included phrases like 'eight kept, two in family':

These advertisements could be useful evidence in the Nazi case that we are a decadent people, and they must foster discontent and suspicion among the poor at home. There is nothing necessarily unpatriotic in a large household staff. Some houses require many workers if they are not to fall in ruins. . . . The wrong is in the suggestion of easy lives offered by the advertised number of family to servants. This is not a time to be offering comfortable corners to trained and efficient workers of any kind.[39]

Other critics, like the MP, Eleanor Rathbone, saw the hogging of servants by selfish mistresses as damaging to the war effort, since wives who had been doing essential work were compelled to abandon it when they had to do all their own household chores. 'Is it fair that selfish women should be allowed, as at present, to have so many manual workers on the excuse that they are below or above the registration age?'[40] Affluent householders even forced up the hourly rates of unskilled dailies to such an extent that they priced out modestly placed but more deserving neighbours.[41]

The government, however, declined to be drawn into the issue of labour 'rationing' beyond the limits envisaged by the compulsory registration schemes. This was made clear in January 1942 when an MP asked about the setting of an official minimum and maximum amount of domestic labour in relation to a 'reasonable standard of household requirements'. In reply the Joint Parliamentary Secretary to the Ministry of Labour and National Service declared that after careful consideration, it had been found impossible 'to lay down hard and fast rules' as to the amount of domestic service to be allowed to households of varying size or composition.[42]

Staff advertisements at this time stressed the advantages an individual employer could offer, such as the location of a post in a 'safe' area away from enemy bombs, or the provision of good accommodation, plentiful outings, convenient access to towns or railway stations and a relatively light work load. There was a tendency to avoid the use of the words 'servant' and 'maid'. Instead there were appeals for 'assistants' or 'helps' – lady helps, mother's helps and useful helps. Typical was an appeal in *The Lady* of 13 February 1941, for a

Domestic help; plain cooking; all duties; help given; comfortable home; family 2-3; country house; safe area; between Bath-Bristol.

The expansion of the home help service in the early 1940s made an attempt to solve the problem of 'hardship' cases by covering, from 1944, the sick, infirm and aged, as well as the nursing and pregnant mothers provided for under the original scheme.[43] By February 1943 home helps were already employed in 150 local authority areas as part of their maternity and child welfare programmes.[44] Employment exchanges began providing both recruits for home help services and domestics for 'hardship' households during 1944. In the first eight months of the year, 11,967 workers were supplied to these groups.[45] Following the creation of the National Health Service in 1948 responsibility for home helps passed to local authority health departments. However, the weaknesses in the recruitment and training of suitable women remained. Another problem was the reluctance of poorer housewives to let outsiders enter their shabby and badly equipped homes, a difficulty that could only be removed by a general improvement in housing conditions.[46]

When the National Health Service was launched in 1948 there were around 11,000 full-time and part-time home helps at work. Twelve years later, some 50,000 women were helping in 300,000 homes and this had increased to 62,097 at work in 1967 – of whom 41,147 worked for county councils, 16,387 for county boroughs and 9,191 for the London boroughs.[47] For the workers themselves, the scheme meant employment under agreed conditions by local authorities, rather than by individual householders. The issue of extracting payment for their services was left to the authority, rather than being a matter of negotiation between the householder and the home help.

During the war some large houses contrived to keep extra staff by offering accommodation to military personnel. Mary Cocking started work at Standen, near East Grinstead, in 1941, when she was fourteen. There were still seven on the staff and she worked mainly in the kitchens. However, as the war progressed and staff numbers dwindled to four, she was 'promoted' to duties in the 'front' of the house, such as looking after the drawing room fire. When the parlourmaid had time off, Mary took over her duties, answering the door and the telephone, as well as the household bells, taking tea into the drawing room and serving dinner at night. For this she wore a smart green dress, and muslin apron and cap supplied by her employer, Miss Beale. Her morning clothes she had to buy herself: 'I remember I made my aprons out of sheets my family gave me as clothes were on "coupons".' She was 'let off doing any war work as we had officers in the medical corps staying at Standen; they went to the Queen Victoria Hospital during the day and back for the evening meal. They came on Monday evening and left Friday morning. We then had to get the rooms ready for the next lot.'[48]

Despite the wartime pressures, discipline at Standen remained strict: 'We had to ask Mrs Last [the housekeeper] for permission to put the radio on. I was never allowed to read a book. I always had to do something that occupied my hands like sewing or knitting.' Occasionally, the cook would take her round the garden when the Beales were away, while at the appropriate season she and some of the other servants went into the kitchen garden to pick soft fruit: 'at that time we had double summer time so at 10 p.m. it was only 8 p.m. by the sun and still light.'[49] Mary remained at Standen until 1951 when she lost a leg in a motor-cycle accident and had to learn to walk again with the aid of crutches and, later, an artificial leg.

She remembered, too, that during the war, rations for the dining room and the servants' hall were supplemented by milk, eggs, rabbits and pheasants from the estate farm and by fresh vegetables from the garden. These benefits were shared by many other country house domestics at that time.

Sheila Chugg was another young, wartime maid, this time in a small Gloucestershire town. Although she had won a scholarship to the grammar school, her parents could not afford to let her go and at fourteen, in 1941, she began work at the home of an elderly solicitor. Her fellow servants were a staid housekeeper in her thirties and an elderly gardener-cum-handyman. Despite the servant shortage, her conditions were little better than those experienced by maids ten or twenty years earlier. She slept in a sparsely furnished, unheated attic room and was paid 10s a month, plus her keep. She was also limited to one weekly bath and had one half-day a week off, from which she had to return by 8 p.m.

Our sitting room was the kitchen, sitting by the old range in winter to keep warm and [we] went to bed at 9 p.m. with a cup of cocoa. My mother told me I would probably be tested for honesty and one morning [I] found a sixpence in the fireplace; which I handed in, but the look on the faces was enough for me to think mother had been right.

During the winter with the blackout in operation all the windows, eleven in all, had to be blacked out. I was a nervous fourteen-year-old . . . and with the housekeeper on her half-day I decided to fix the blackouts early while it was still reasonably light. I did not relish going around the large old house with just a small glimmer from a partially lit torch. That evening Mr H. left his office early and he came into the house and roared out, 'Who has done this? Remove them at once.' This I did and then had to go around later in the dark fixing them all again. It was not easy either, especially on the stairs when I had to reach a high window. I really thought one day I would fall to the bottom of the stairs.[50]

This treatment reinforced Sheila's general dislike of service and after a year she left to become a railway booking clerk. There she stayed for eight years and 'enjoyed every minute of it'. When she gave in her notice, her solicitor employer declared dismissively: 'Oh! I suppose you're going there just to stick stamps on envelopes.' A replacement maid was found almost at once. Like Sheila, she was a fourteen-year-old school leaver, but she seemed to find domestic work more congenial than her predecessor had done.[51]

By 1943, the unpopularity of domestic service applied not merely to private households, but, more seriously, to hospitals and other public institutions. Concern over the shortage of hospital domestics became so acute that in the spring of 1943 Violet Markham was invited to draw up a remedial scheme. She suggested the formation of a domestic service corps, which would function rather like a military or Land Army unit and would offer prospects of promotion and improved status to members. Even so, Miss Markham doubted whether it would revive what she described as this 'often despised form of employment'. An essential part of the status-building process was the provision of a suitable uniform:

> In a world of great and tragic events the call of duty should, you may think, suffice without any adventitious appeal for clothes. One has, however, to take facts and people as they are. . . . A uniform is a factor of great psychological importance if the Corps is to achieve one of its objects – that of raising the status of domestic workers. In a uniform a ward maid will carry her head as high as her friend in the Forces; an arm band or a badge will have no such effect.[52]

If the Corps were successful it could be extended to other labour-starved public institutions which satisfied its basic requirements concerning 'work and wages as well as supervision, training and a field of promotion'.[53]

In the end, the formation of a Domestic Service Corps proved impractical, partly because of the government's inability to provide suitable uniforms at a time of shortages.[54] It was impossible to 'direct' women into hospital domestic work, because there was still no basic framework of conditions of service covering wages, hours and similar matters. That was remedied by the appointment of the Hetherington Committee in 1943 to draw up a temporary scheme covering pay and employment conditions. It was to be replaced by a formal National Joint Council, such as already existed in some other industries, as soon as possible. Violet Markham was sceptical about its prospects: 'I am afraid the "welfare" carrot has been dangled before the nose of too many donkeys to produce any sort of a thrill!' Nevertheless, as a result of the Hetherington Report women were directed into hospital domestic service from 1944 to the end of 1945, with 34,211 women placed in this sector by the Ministry of Labour during the first eight months of 1944; 2,287 men were also directed to domestic work in these institutions. However, the problem of staff wastage persisted and during the first six months of 1944 the net increase in full-time domestic staff in hospitals and similar institutions was only about 5,500.[55]

After the war the promised National Joint Council agreement was drawn up, offering, for the first time, national minimum rates of pay and conditions of service for domestic staff in hospitals. By now domestics were accepted as an essential part of the patient care team and in 1946 a book published by the King Edward's Hospital Fund for London placed much emphasis on the importance of good amenities for them, to ensure they were aware that their contribution to the patients' well-being was 'valued at its true worth'.[56]

In the meantime, broader governmental anxieties over the future of private domestic service led to the appointment in March 1944 of Violet Markham and Florence Hancock to report on the sector for the Minister of Labour. Miss Hancock, the national organiser for women in the Transport and General Workers' Union, had helped to prepare a Memorandum on the Post-War Position of the Domestic Worker in the spring of 1943. This drew attention to the way in which former servants were helping the war effort in the armed forces, munition factories, civil defence, transport and other important spheres. 'These workers who are now serving their country so well, are deserving of better conditions in their old employment, when the war ends.'[57] The task of the Markham-Hancock team was to evaluate reform proposals and to draw up a plan for future action.

The report was completed in July 1944, but was only published, after some prodding from Miss Markham, in the summer of 1945. It pinpointed current weaknesses in the occupation, but stressed her conviction that with proper organisation, domestic work could become 'entirely honourable and self-respecting . . . for any woman', as well as performing an essential community service and providing 'excellent training for the girl who subsequently marries and has a home of her own'. The problems of employers were recognised too, particularly those of working-class women with large families, for whom home helps could provide assistance, and of middle-class wives looking after 'an old-fashioned house with stone passages, coal fires and an antiquated range'. Without domestic aid not only were such women overworked, but they were prevented from taking any constructive part in central or local government, or from following a professional career. Instead they had to concentrate on home duties. Finally, there was the demographic effect:

> it is idle to preach the need for a higher birth rate if home life is to spell undiluted drudgery for the wife and mother. The demand of the girl who has had a modern education, for personal liberty and self expression is much too strong for any acceptance of an existence wholly circumscribed by home work.[58]

In the report's view, the need to solve the domestic service problem was inextricably linked to the 'future of the home, that cornerstone of the national life'.

It was essentially a class and gender-based analysis of the situation. Housework was seen as women's work and working-class women were to be persuaded to come forward as servants in order that, in the main, middle-class wives could pursue professional careers or take part in political life. This was a theme to which Violet Markham was to return over the years.[59] The working-class wife and mother was merely to have access to home helps, on a short-term basis, to enable her to cope with emergencies.

If the necessary servants were to be recruited, training standards had to be improved, in order to raise the occupation's status. In many ways this was a reiteration of views put forward after the First World War to popularise domestic work, but unlike the earlier initiatives, Markham-Hancock suggested formal machinery to achieve the desired end. The National Institute of Houseworkers (NIH) was set up to provide training, certification and agreed conditions of employment at wages that would apply, initially, to its own graduates, but which would, it was hoped, also influence other domestic employment.[60]

Another possibility to cover the shortfall, although one not mentioned by Markham-Hancock, was the recruitment of foreign servants and *au pairs*. This began in 1945, with the securing of a few hundred Belgian women for domestic work in hospitals, but became of major importance after 1946.

The Ministry of Labour also put pressure on women to enter private service in 1945, in some cases by threatening to withdraw unemployment benefit. As a result, around 25,000 women were placed in 'hardship households'. But despite these campaigns, the post-war servant deficit persisted. The opportunities for females to work in better-paid, higher status and more varied occupations elsewhere hampered those anxious to persuade them to take up household employment. This even applied to children's homes, which at first were attacked for failing to develop the talents of female residents by continuing to prepare them for domestic work.[61] At Dr Barnardo's in 1946, 86 of the 176 girls leaving the homes went as 'general house assistants', with a further 9 going as domestic hospital staff, 10 as cooks and 12 as nursemaids.[62] However, the girls were increasingly reluctant to take up these careers and by 1952 Barnardo's had ceased to train youngsters for paid household employment.[63]

This did not stop some of the charity's supporters from demanding they supply servants. In October 1947, Lady Blackford, who was a regular subscriber, called the shortage of maids 'the most crying need of the day and one of the most desirable in the interest of girl children . . . yet because of idle nonsense . . . not half of your girls are thus prepared. I have of late tried to get a young girl from the Homes without the slightest success.'[64] A Barnardo official responded soothingly by stating that although 'most girls would be much better off in domestic service', they themselves preferred to train for other employment. He added that in 1946 Barnardo's had received 250 applications for every female servant placed.

At a time when great stress was placed on the need to boost population growth, concerns about birth rates continued to be voiced. In February 1946 a young mother wrote angrily to *The Times*, pointing out she had a child of two, a husband overseas and no domestic help of any kind:

In common with most of our friends we are quite prepared
to have a family of at least four children, provided we have
adequate help at reasonable wages. . . . The local Labour
Exchange and servants' agency have yielded no one after
weeks of dogged inquiry; my advertisements brought forth
one reply from a cook who asked £3 10s a week and a
private sitting-room.

Either we young mothers must have home helps at a
sensible wage . . . or else the government must accept the
fact that we will simply have to forgo all hopes of a family
exceeding, at the very outside, three children. There is a limit
after all to what the human frame can tackle.[65]

Other critics, like Angus Maude and Roy Lewis, pointed
to the many people who felt life was 'scarcely worth living
unless it is civilized (as distinct from mechanised).' To
them, this meant having 'a modest amount of domestic
service. . . . [I]f good furniture, good silver and good
pictures (all ofwhich need careful maintenance) are to
be banished . . . to museums; and if entertaining is to
be permanently restricted . . . then emigration to Eire
or South Africa seems the only hope'.[66] Presumably in
those two destinations it was felt plenty of domestic help
could be found. It was an exaggerated example of a fairly
common upper middle-class view that home life without
servants was intolerable.

For some, the remedy lay in the employment of 'dailies'
for a few hours a day or a week. Significantly, the number of

charwomen and office cleaners in England and Wales jumped from 140,146 in 1931 to 215,336 twenty years later; by 1961 it had reached around 317,400.[67] As Margaret Powell recalled, during these years women 'didn't have to worry about references on a daily job. You just said you'd never been out before, or, that the people you last worked for had died.'[68] But even at this time the increased use of contract cleaning for offices and institutions attracted many 'dailies' who wished to avoid the fraught personal relationships that often went with private service.

More optimistically, there was a wider acceptance of the benefits of labour-saving appliances. In 1949 a new edition of *Mrs Beeton's Household Management* noted that the shortage of domestic staff and the high wages they demanded had forced many wives to take on more housework themselves. In that context, labour-saving devices were of major importance, even if some of them, at first sight, seemed expensive: 'the labour they save will soon make the housewife appreciate how economical they really are. And it must be remembered that they are saving servants' wages as well.'[69] In the long run a wider use of domestic appliances would overcome many household difficulties and some former servant-keepers came to welcome their new independence. An Elstree householder wrote in August 1974:

I am a good butler, my wife is the best cook I've ever met. We both of us drive a car very much better than my grandmother's old chauffeur. . . . Now that we do all these things for ourselves we do them much better.[70]

Similarly, Lady Mander admitted she did not regret the loss of staff as a result of the war: 'It is a relief now not to have to try to keep up appearances or to guard one's speech at meals or to catch hostile glances from the gardener for picking a flower instead of waiting for him to bring plants in from the hothouse.'[71]

Where full-time domestics were employed, their long-term commitment to a single family was no longer expected. Even prestigious Norland nurses rarely stayed on once the children were nearing school age. High taxation, which reduced parental incomes and the larger salaries expected by staff meant that 'the very best nurse' was 'regarded as a luxury'.[72]

Staff also had to demonstrate versatility in their domestic skills rather than pursue the specialist approach which had applied, particularly in large households, in the 1930s. A butler, writing in 1950, described how he and the cook-housekeeper looked after their employer's country house:

> sometimes I go to London to do some cleaning and polishing in the flat and offices of my employer. . . . Besides the work of the house, I can find time to mow the lawns, look after the hens . . . and drive the small car. . . . Since I have been single handed, we have sent all the ornamental silver . . .

rose bowls, loving cups, etc, to the jewellers to be lacquered. This has been a great success . . . and the silver looks as if it were cleaned by a butler every day. . . . Lacquering . . . saves hours in cleaning copper coal scuttles, antique brass fenders, and all the hundred and one things that had formerly to be cleaned each week.[73]

Arthur Inch, when he returned to service in the mid-1950s, found himself 'covering the jobs of ten men in the pantry. . . . As well as being butler/valet I also did a few chauffeuring jobs such as taking the children to school. . . . For a while we had a temporary daily cook in and then a couple were engaged as cook and gardener. . . . My wife did lady's maid duty and any visiting ladies. A local girl on the estate also came in to do housework. After a couple of years the married couple departed . . . and we then had a cook who came in for week-ends only.' Soon after he decided to take a post as single-handed butler to a titled family, but on discovering that his employers were heavy drinkers, he quickly moved, to become a butler/valet/chauffeur: 'but chauffeuring children to school and washing cars, etc. was interfering too much with my indoor work so after a year I left there.' The other staff comprised a chef and his wife and a couple of dailies for the housework. Then in 1960 he saw an advertisement for a butler/valet's job in Sussex, for the Kleinwort family. He applied and was appointed. He remained there as single-handed butler-valet for the next twenty years, with his wife doing a few hours weekly as a housemaid and looking after and mending the household linen. There was a full-time cook and two charwomen from the estate to do the cleaning.[74]

Staff in other large country houses had similar experiences after 1945. A long-serving butler at a substantial property in south Leicestershire claimed in the mid-1980s that he could not name a place in the whole county with two full-time resident servants, while another Leicestershire butler, who began as a footman at Quenby Hall in 1949, declared: 'Footmen almost died out with me. In later years they wanted a butler-valet or a chauffeur-valet, we started merging jobs.'[75] As the columns of *The Lady* showed, by the late 1950s advertisements for domestic help had increased sharply compared to the low point reached immediately after the Second World War. However, the emphasis was on cooks, nannies and mother's helps, rather than on the wide range of staff that had been at work before 1939.[76]

Inevitably, these changes and the need for economy to meet a growing tax burden, led to modifications in the lifestyles of stately home owners. Some, like the aged Lady Airlie, left their residence and moved to a hotel.[77] Others, like the Earl and Countess of Crawford and Balcarres, concluded they could not maintain more than one property. Immediately after the war they disposed of their English estate and settled at Balcarres in Scotland.

Our household varied in numbers over the years – sometimes we had foreign couples, mad cooks and bad cooks, an ex-housemaid married to an ex-footman who remained with us as a couple till they retired. The head gardener's wife, who came as cook, was with us for eleven years and though a good cook was a woman of uncertain temper and very jealous. When she departed in a huff and took her reluctant husband with her, the relief was enormous. Two dailies then came to our rescue with the housework, and I took on the cooking, and, if the house was full, got outside help. . . . Hoovers took the place of brooms and mops in the housemaids' cupboards on every floor and wash basins in bedrooms meant no more carrying of hot water cans. . . . There was always a lot to do, but I for one never regretted that I was not a 'châtelaine' of a large household.[78]

Increasingly, as with Chatsworth and Woburn Abbey, houses were opened to the public, partly for tax purposes and partly to boost income. At Chatsworth, once the girls' public school that had occupied it during the war had moved out in 1946, the house was left empty except for two housemaids who 'perched in a distant room at the north end'. The sheer number of girls had made everything look shabby and the lack of domestic staff meant it was impossible to keep clean. Eventually, in 1948 the then Duke and Duchess of Devonshire decided to reopen the house. They engaged two redoubtable Hungarian sisters, Ilona and Elisabeth Solymossy, as cook and housemaid and asked them 'to gather up a team of their acquaintances who were sturdy enough to face the enormous task of cleaning and making ready the house for the opening'. In all, eleven Hungarians arrived and worked through the winter of 1948-9, so that the house was ready to receive the public at Easter 1949. Despite petrol rationing '75,000 people came to see it at half a crown each and a shilling for the garden'.[79] In November 1950, however, the 10th Duke died and there were heavy death duties to pay. Not until the mid-1950s did the eleventh Duke and Duchess decide to move to Chatsworth themselves. There then followed a major refurbishment, presided over by the Solymossy sisters with as much energy as they had displayed in setting the public part of the house in order a decade earlier.[80] The Duke and Duchess finally returned in 1959. As the Duchess recalled, during the 1950s the Hungarians continued to clean, mend, scrub, polish and tidy. 'Sometimes they brought forth wonders that had lain beneath other wonders in hopeless heaps of *things* in attic room after attic room. They made order out of disorder.'[81]

At Woburn Abbey, the 13th Duke of Bedford found an almost derelict property when he inherited the estate at the beginning of the 1950s. After much hard work it too was opened to the public in 1955. However, it was very different from his grandfather's day in 1940, when there were still fifty or sixty indoor servants employed. Soon after the public opening, the Duke described the way he and the Duchess ran their own wing at Woburn:

Where my grandfather had scores of servants in Belgrave Square and at the Abbey, we made do with seven, to cover both houses, with all the public engagements that the stately-home business entails. We do have fourteen dailies and six night-watchmen who come in on a part-time basis from Woburn village, but their job is to clean and look after the whole vast complex of the house, including the public rooms and the tea-room and restaurant in the stables.[82]

Outside similar modifications of pre-war practice were apparent. At Aynho the army finally left in 1947 and the task of renovation began. Badly damaged box hedges that surrounded the flower beds near the mansion were rooted out and a simple design of eight beds, each surrounded with new box hedges, was substituted. Many pre-war methods of cultivation for the kitchen garden were abandoned because of labour shortages. As Ted Humphris noted, a motor plough and cultivators were used instead of spades and rakes. 'The war years had certainly hastened the end of the old methods of cultivating and running a garden.' By the early 1950s Aynho Park House and its pleasure grounds were open to the public and once again Humphris provided flowers to decorate the house.[83] However, it was very different from the spacious hospitality that had prevailed in 1939.

Even wealthy landowners like the Wernhers at Luton Hoo and Lord Leconfield at Petworth became more economical in the post-war years. At Luton Hoo, the garden labour force was financed by selling some of the produce at Covent Garden market each week. That meant one of the gardeners going up to London with vegetables and plants, the latter being sold to leading florists in South Audley Street. Bob Gregory had this task, but he came to dislike the new spirit of commercialism. After two years he moved as head gardener to Bitham Hall, Avon Dassett, in Warwickshire, where there were two small kitchen gardens, a greenhouse block and a large plant house. The property had been neglected during the war, but after twelve months' energetic effort it began to take shape once more. Bob remained about three years before he moved to a higher paid job. There followed a brief and unhappy spell as head gardener at the Kesteven Farm Institute in Lincolnshire, before he became head gardener at Maidwell Hall, Northamptonshire, then a preparatory school. With four under-gardeners, he had to grow enough vegetables and fruit to supply the staff, pupils and domestic helpers – a total of about 110 people. Flowers, too, were, raised, while the pleasure grounds, lake, rock gardens and playing fields had to be kept in good order. Nevertheless, Gregory adapted to the new situation and remained at Maidwell until the mid-1970s.[84]

At Petworth, too, there were great changes. Whereas thirty-six men had once worked in the gardens, by the end of the war that had dropped to just three, including the head gardener, Fred Streeter. In 1950 staff numbers recovered to nine, but despite a sharp reduction in the acreage of the private gardens, this was still inadequate. One of the stud grooms mowed the lawns and any surplus produce was sold. Where once the cultivated area and grounds had covered 300 acres, in 1950 that had shrunk to fifteen.[85]

In the 1944-5 *Report on the Post-War Organisation of Private Domestic Employment*, Violet Markham and Florence Hancock had concluded optimistically that 'I serve' was a 'princely motto'. However, in the post-war world, with a changed economic and social climate, it became increasingly difficult to persuade people to accept that concept. One means proposed in the report, at least with regards to the women, was the setting up of the National Institute of Houseworkers. The aim was to train efficient domestic staff and at the same time, by the award of diplomas and the drawing up of a code of working conditions, to raise the status of the occupation. In future, declared contemporary newspapers, there would be 'no more servants in Britain, only house workers'.[86]

THE ROLE OF THE NATIONAL INSTITUTE OF HOUSEWORKERS

The Markham-Hancock report was published in the summer of 1945, but it was February of the following year before the Minister of Labour and National Service announced that the government had decided to set up the National Institute of Houseworkers (NIH) along lines recommended in the report. The Institute was formally incorporated as a non-profit-making company in June 1946 and in the following month a board of directors was appointed to manage its affairs. As Dorothy Elliott, who chaired the board in its early days, put it, the scheme had 'two main aims: to turn out a domestic worker skilled in her craft; and to give to that worker a sense of confidence in herself as a member of the community, breaking down the idea that domestic workers are a race apart.'[87] To that end, a broad training programme was drawn up, combining general and health education with practical domestic instruction, so that students would not only become skilled houseworkers but 'good citizens' who knew 'how to make good use of their leisure'.[88]

The institute began work early in 1947 with three principal tasks. These were the establishment of a diploma examination which could be taken by experienced workers, as well as by the newly trained; the creation of an instruction programme at NIH residential centres, where students would be taught free of charge and would also receive a small maintenance grant; and the provision of employment for successful candidates at the end of their course under terms set out by the institute and agreed with employers. These covered wages, working hours, leisure time and other general issues. It was realised that a statutory code of conditions for private domestic employment was impracticable, since that would have involved inspection of homes to ensure that the conditions were being observed, but it was hoped NIH standards would influence employers generally.[89] The main concern, however, was to ensure the training was of a sufficiently high quality to raise the standing of the occupation and thereby attract more workers to it.[90]

The NIH also undertook to recruit day helpers, who would be employed directly by local committees. They would work for individual householders on an hourly basis and could be full or part time. They were to be paid by the local committees, which would then recoup their expenses by charging householders the relatively high sum of 2s 6d an hour. That covered the worker's pay, her national insurance contribution and the administrative costs of the scheme. In many respects these women fulfilled a similar role to that of the local authority home helps, but under the aegis of the NIH rather than of a public body.[91]

The standards set by the NIH for resident domestics included agreed pay rates; a working timetable of ninety-six hours per fortnight, beyond which overtime became payable; the provision of a bed-sitting room or a separate bedroom and sitting room with heating; the granting of three half-days a week free time; a fortnight's paid annual holiday for the first five years of service, with three weeks thereafter; and opportunities for the servant to entertain her friends out of working hours.[92] In many respects this reflected the programme put forward by the National Union of Domestic Workers in its *Steps* document during the autumn of 1938.

The NIH was financed by government grants and loans. Thus, in the year ended 31 March 1949, grants of £75,637 were made, plus loans of around £77,000 to cover the acquisition and equipment of the training centres and other projects. The following year, ending 31 March 1950, Ministry of Labour grants totalled £113,935, with a further £22,000 by way of loans.[93] Yet, despite this expenditure, the training programme was slow to develop and some early centres were very small. That opened at Oxford in the autumn of 1947, for example, was set up in a Victorian villa and by September 1948 had just fourteen students, six of whom resided on the premises. They attended a local technical school for lessons in English and for extra tuition in cookery, laundry work and sewing. First aid and general health instruction was given at a nearby Red Cross station.[94] Perhaps not surprisingly, the Oxford centre closed in August 1950, with its students transferred to new, larger premises at Harrow.[95]

The first centre, opened at Chilton Cantelo House, near Yeovil, was more ambitious. In January 1948 it had thirty students, aged from fifteen to fifty-one. Domestic training took place at the centre itself, with the students performing all the chores as well as learning household skills. Leisure activities included community singing and play-reading and there was a weekly class in Civics at the Yeovil Technical School.[96] This accorded with the NIH's avowed aim of providing trainees with a 'full and interesting life'.[97]

By late 1949 a total of nine centres were in operation, with places for 365 students; 327 students had completed courses, of whom 173 were adults and 154 juveniles.[98] But juveniles (those under seventeen) soon outstripped adult entrants, comprising about 70 per cent of those entering between September 1947 and 31 October 1950.[99] They were recruited with the help of the Youth Employment Service. This preponderance of young people doubtless encouraged the NIH to be more authoritarian in its approach than might otherwise have been the case. Around two-thirds of the trainees' time was devoted to practical instruction, with a further one-fifth taken up with general education. The rest of the course involved practical work in selected private households. For those aged seventeen and above the course lasted six months and at the end they took the qualifying examination which gave associate membership of the institute. For juveniles a nine-month course was arranged. After this they went out as pre-diploma students to spend a year working in a household chosen by the NIH, before returning to sit their examination.[100]

In order to develop the wider interests of the younger students, each was supplied with a special notebook when she left the centre for her pre-diploma year. In it she was to enter points of interest in her job, comments on any further education course she took, a list of books she had read and information about the area where she was working.[101]

Sheila Chapman went to Chilton Cantelo when she left school, aged fifteen, in 1949. The trainees were housed in dormitories and despite the reluctance of many pre-war maids to wear caps, their uniform consisted of a cap and overall. Most girls were homesick at first, 'but the teachers were very good. . . . They were very strict on keeping our rooms tidy and clean, and we had inspection of lockers regularly.'[102] Sheila's first residential placement was in the household of a local vicar, where she spent about a month. Her friend went to a nearby doctor: 'It was quite lonely there, looking back I think it could have been cheap labour.' At the end of the nine-month course she went on a one-year placement to the home of a store manager in Plymouth, where she carried out housework, baby sitting and laundry: 'we were supposed to have gone to college for half a day, I'm afraid I didn't attend.' She had limited time off – just Tuesday and Saturday afternoons each week. This was below the standard stipulated by the NIH. Yet, despite the hard work, she was happy. Unlike many servants, especially those before 1939, she was treated as part of the family and had her meals with the rest of the household, rather than in the kitchen. When the year was up, she returned to Chilton Cantelo to take her examination and on completing this successfully, returned to the placement family. There she remained until her marriage in September 1954.[103] NIH reports suggest that a high proportion of trainees stayed with their first employer. The institute considered this confirmed the care with which mistress and maid were matched by its training officers.[104]

Most successful candidates, however, took the examination as 'experienced' workers rather than as trainees like Sheila Chapman. Even in December 1960, when the NIH had been running for over a decade, only 1,537 of the 5,287 holders of the diploma had followed a training course. When compared with the census returns it also indicated the limited success of a scheme intended to boost the domestic labour force. In 1951, there were 724,000 domestic workers recorded, of whom 178,000 were resident servants in private homes. In 1931 there had been an estimated 707,000 servants resident in private homes out of a domestic labour force of about 1.3 million.[105]

It may be asked why experienced workers took the diploma examination, especially as they had to pay an entrance fee. For this there seem to be two explanations. First, some maids were anxious to have the status of certificated workers – something which NIH propaganda stressed. In the May 1948 issue of *The Houseworker*, the institute's journal, several successful candidates gave their reasons for seeking qualifications. One, who had been a domestic for seven years, thought 'it established a guarantee of my experience and also that it would be a very nice thing to have. The Diploma and Badge are two of my proudest possessions and I am now not ashamed to say I am a domestic worker.' Another woman, employed as a cook-housekeeper for a semi-invalid, felt she had 'a trump card to use', should she need to find fresh employment.

The diploma was also an advantage for those recruited as local authority home helps or as day workers for NIH local committees. Indeed, for day workers it was a necessity. From an early stage, the London County Council encouraged its home helps to become qualified and the age range of candidates examined was from twenty-three to sixty-two years. A number of other authorities followed suit, including Oxford, Newcastle upon Tyne, Preston and Essex County Council.[106] Even when there was no formal policy of encouraging staff to take the examination (and unfortunately for the long-term success of the NIH, that was true of the majority of authorities) additional payments might be made to qualified staff. This was Sheila Chapman's experience when, a few years after marriage, she began working for the Cornish Home Help Service, in the early 1960s.[107]

But while girls like Sheila found the NIH and its courses attractive, outsiders pinpointed its deficiencies. A visitor to Chilton Cantelo in 1948-9 compared its spartan atmosphere to that of an 'old-fashioned "reformatory school"'. The principal was described as 'an ideal matron

of a "toughs school"'. Apart from that 'the rooms were
. . . very cold where the girls were sewing etc.'[108] Still
more damaging were accusations of extravagance in the
running of the training programmes. These were taken
up in the press and by MPs like Angus Maude. He noted
that during the year 1949-50 about 290 students had
been trained at a total cost of almost £114,000, plus
£22,000 in loans:

> I find it difficult . . . to believe that the primary aim of the
> Institute, which is to raise the status of domestic service, can
> be achieved by turning out some 300 trained students a year,
> not by any means all of whom will be going into private
> domestic service, when the majority of people have probably
> never heard of the Institute, and when the attractions of
> domestic service as a trade are not being widely disseminated
> through the good offices of the Institute.[109]

In December 1952, another MP questioned the Minister
of Labour on the cost of publishing *The Houseworker*
and upon the size of its circulation. He was told that in
the year ending 31 March 1952, there had been a loss
of £600 on its publication. Of 4,000 copies of each issue
printed around half were sold and from the rest 'a free
distribution is made to representative bodies interested
in women's employment'.[110]

Underlying the debates was the dismissive approach
of the *Manchester Guardian*, which in September 1951

found it was hardly necessary 'to maintain residential training colleges for housework', especially as up to July of that year only 834 girls had completed courses at the centres. About a fifth of them had subsequently married or given up paid domestic work:

> Training is expensive and seems to be becoming more so. The Committee of Public Accounts was told last year that it cost about £130 a girl; the Ministry of Labour's latest figure is 'approximately £160' for girls over seventeen and 'about £200' for younger girls, who do a longer course. . . . Could not more training be arranged in hospitals and other institutions, where the work even of beginners could be of immediate value? Whether it is worth maintaining the institute on its present scale is a question that merits careful study.[111]

To such critics the NIH replied that in the long term it was important to develop the general knowledge and self-confidence of the trainees, and it was working towards making domestic work 'as natural, dignified and honourable as . . . teaching, nursing, administration, agriculture or industry' .[112] The *Manchester Guardian* argued that such improvement in the 'status' of servants as had occurred was more the result of post-war full employment and the consequent competition for domestic help than the influence of the NIH. The institute itself ruefully admitted the attack had been harmful.

Against this background and following the election of a cost-cutting Conservative government in 1951, the NIH's grant was reduced by almost two-thirds in 1952.[113] This meant only one of the nine training centres, that at Harrow, could be retained. However, the Bridge of Allan Centre in Scotland survived as a result of a grant from the Scottish Association for Homecraft Training, a voluntary body grant-aided by the Scottish Education Department, and the Swansea centre reopened after a brief gap, as a result of financial support from local education authorities in Wales and England.[114]

The NIH also had difficulties with its Daily Houseworker Service, which had opened in Portsmouth in 1948 and was eventually to be taken up in seventeen other towns throughout Great Britain. Part of the problem lay in the hourly payment of 2s 6d required for the workers. That was higher than the amount normally paid to charwomen. As a result, householders were reluctant to recruit them or if they were engaged, they were often expected to do a good deal of heavy work during their spell on duty. Staff turnover was rapid and some workers entered into private arrangements with families whom they had first contacted under the NIH. Any local service which failed to pay for itself was closed down.[115] In 1954 a peak of over 500 employees were servicing some 2,000 households each week, but that had fallen to 329 workers by 1960-1. They were helping 1,055 households a week.[116] Four years later the totals had dropped to 266 workers assisting 870 householders. By then the scheme was largely irrelevant at a time when local authority home helps in England and Wales numbered around 62,000. In 1966 the service was closed down. Significantly, too, of home helps surveyed a year later, only one in five had received training of any kind and nearly one-third of the courses they had taken had lasted for just half a day.[117] Despite the institute's repeated efforts to offer special courses to home helps, in this sphere, too, it had failed to make an impact.

Disagreements arose over NIH requirements that a full-time residential maid in private service should work a basic ninety-six hours per fortnight and should be free from domestic duties at other times, unless she agreed to put in extra hours, when overtime would be payable. Some mistresses felt that while a girl was on the premises, perhaps reading or sewing in her room, she should be available for work.[118] But the NIH maintained that although give and take between the parties was desirable, it was important to establish that when the worker was 'off duty', she should be 'free to stay in the house, which is her home, as well as her place of employment, without having duties . . . imposed upon her'.[119] It was, of course, this problem of off duty hours within the home that had irked so many resident maids before 1939. The institute argued that as other occupations had 'limited and regular hours and time off', so should domestic employment.[120] The difficulty lay in persuading mistresses that such 'trade union' attitudes were as appropriate within the house as they were outside it.

A final obstacle to the NIH's success was the disintegration of the domestic world for which it had been created. Not only did the new spirit of female independence and egalitarianism make the employment of domestic help less attractive to many wives, but the advent of modern, labour-saving houses and new electrical appliances made their recruitment less necessary. In the 'swinging sixties' traditional bourgeois values were rejected and less store was placed on having immaculately maintained rooms. Instead, families preferred to spend their spare cash on cars, entertainment, holidays and various new consumer durables.

Potential servants, for their part, were sceptical of institute claims that they were entering a skilled occupation which was of vital importance to the well-being of the community. Private service was especially unpopular and those who trained as domestics preferred to take institutional posts in hospitals, schools and similar establishments or to work in hotels. In 1964-5, the NIH's annual report pointed out that the trend towards institutional work was increasing and that 54 per cent of first placements were in this type of employment.[121] By September 1970 that had risen to 80 per cent of placements; only 20 per cent were now in private households.[122] Figures produced by the institute in June 1972 suggested not more than about eighty of its associate members were still in private service.[123]

From the early 1950s, the government seemed to lose interest in the scheme. Following the economy drive of

1952, there was a threat four years later to withdraw the grant altogether. Only after vigorous protests and lengthy negotiations was that changed to an annual sum of £15,000 to be devoted to organising the diploma examinations only. All other work, including the running of the Harrow training centre, was to be financed from outside sources.[124]

Over the years the grant slowly increased, to reach £37,000 by 1970-1, but throughout the period the NIH was starved of cash.[125] Its role diminished further and it was forced to diversify, offering training packages to various organisations, often on a short-term basis only. In 1963, it changed its name to the National Institute for Housecraft, but even in the late 1950s it was already offering brief specialist programmes. These included residential courses at Harrow for the Industrial Welfare Society, the National Society for the Prevention of Cruelty to Children, and the Women's Royal Army Corps. Non-residential training was given to hospital domestic workers.[126] By the mid-1960s these additional activities included a course for Hospital Domestic Forewomen, with over 300 hospital domestic supervisors trained and examined in the period to the end of December 1970.[127] Supervisory courses were organised for hotel staff and were eligible for grants from the Hotel and Catering Industrial Training Board.[128]

The desperate efforts by the NIH to remain afloat were an admission that its original aim of reforming and reviving private domestic service did not match the realities of home life for most British people. Even the diploma lost its modest appeal, with just 186 candidates examined between April 1964 and March 1965. Of these 125 had received residential training. Two years later, the number of candidates examined had fallen to 137; 111 had received training at one of the three surviving centres, while 3 were local authority candidates from Further Education courses and 17 were hospital forewomen.[129]

For its part, the NIH blamed the parsimony of successive governments for its plight. Early in 1971 it complained that since 1956 'the training aspect of the Institute charged as a standard-setting body for domestic employment was not grant-aided although an integral part of standard-setting and examinations. . . . [The] Government's bargain with the Institute has been unusually hard over the last few years. All the modest profits the Institute has made from running outside courses are set against the grant rather than put to use to build up the . . . small reserves.'[130] It pointed out, too, that in 1969 of 4,443 girls aged fifteen to seventeen who had entered catering, hotels and similar services, a mere 746 had taken jobs which provided planned training. This, it argued, highlighted the inadequacy of job training for women and girls in that particular sphere and the need for its own particular expertise.

The comments were provoked by the fact that soon after taking office in 1970 the new Conservative Government began a critical appraisal of NIH activities and funding. After more than a year of deliberation, in December 1971 it announced that the Institute would have to close. It was noted that local education authorities and the major employers of domestic workers, such as hospitals and hotels, had developed training programmes which largely replaced those offered by the NIH. 'Last year some 203 people took the housecraft diploma whereas 6,250 candidates took courses of similar type in other institutions, so the size of the task has got out of all proportion.'[131]

After further negotiations it was agreed in the autumn of 1972 that the Swansea training centre would be taken over by the local authority and incorporated into the Swansea College of Further Education. Students at the Swansea centre would be awarded a certificate issued by the Welsh Joint Education Committee.[132] The rest of the NIH's activities were closed down and the organisation went into voluntary liquidation. Despite all efforts, its aim of ensuring that domestic employment was recognised as 'a worthwhile job and career . . . requiring proper training skills and adequate rewards' remained unfulfilled.[133] Domestic service was still the Cinderella occupation it had always been.

THE FOREIGN CONTRIBUTION

Even before the end of the Second World War, government concern over the inadequate domestic staffing of hospitals had led to attempts to recruit workers from elsewhere in Europe. In March 1945 a Ministry of Labour minute noted there were five thousand domestic vacancies in hospitals. A month later 'useful' contacts had been established with Belgian officials to consider the feasibility of recruiting girls from Belgium for employment in London hospitals. Further meetings followed in London in June and at these a spokesman for the Belgian delegation declared their willingness 'to do all they could to help London in her difficulties realising as they did that Belgium owed its freedom to the stand made by Britain in 1940'.[134]

Agreement was eventually reached to allow Belgian volunteers, mainly between twenty-one and forty-five, to work in London hospitals for periods of at least six months, under clearly established terms regarding pay and working conditions. The first party arrived in July 1945, with the Ministry of Labour, through its Welfare Department, making arrangements to ensure the well-being of the volunteers. The amount of work this involved was later described by a Ministry of Labour official as 'amazing'.[135] In all, 880 women and girls came to Britain under this arrangement, with the last party arriving early in 1946.

Despite its limitations, the scheme was successful. But efforts to extend it to other allied and neutral countries in Europe, including France, Switzerland and Scandinavia, proved fruitless, either because of their own shortage of domestic staff or because of an unwillingness among the women themselves to work in hospitals.[136] As a result, the Ministry of Labour turned its attention to the possible recruitment of volunteers from among the refugees in Displaced Persons Camps in the British zones in Germany and Austria. Already in May 1946 the merits of this option were being discussed. It was pointed out that these were being maintained at British taxpayers' expense and yet they had 'little or no future prospects', at least in the short run, of getting a secure home and employment. In consequence it was likely they would be 'only too glad to accept employment of any kind' in Britain. They were to be recruited for particularly unattractive domestic work in sanatoria and tuberculosis hospitals, with plans drawn up to despatch the first one thousand volunteers as soon as possible.[137] Initially they were to come from the Baltic states of Latvia, Estonia and Lithuania, under an arrangement poetically labelled the 'Balt Cygnet' scheme.[138] They were to be granted entry for one year only, but it was accepted that, given their situation, their permits would probably have to be extended indefinitely, so that they eventually became permanent residents in Britain. Only if they broke the terms of their contract or misbehaved in some other way would they be returned to the Displaced Persons Camps from which they had come.[139]

Despite its opportunistic nature, which took advantage of the plight of the refugees, the venture was successful. In all 2,575 Baltic women had come to Britain in this way by the early months of 1947. This success and the continuing need for domestic workers led the government to extend its recruitment campaign to cover a wider range of Displaced Persons from camps in Germany and Austria, including those outside the British zones. From the spring of 1947 a new European Volunteer Workers scheme called 'Westward Ho' came into operation, which was merged with the earlier Balt Cygnet initiative.[140] In total, 8,170 Displaced Persons were brought over to Britain in 1947 to work in hospitals and similar public institutions or in 'hardship' households. A further 2,250 men and 3,430 women came in as European volunteers in 1948. By the end of 1949 it was announced that 5,200 men and 12,400 females had come to work in hospitals, hostels and other public institutions and in 'hardship' households since the inception of the Balt Cygnet scheme in 1946. A further 870 volunteers came in during 1950, before the 'Westward Ho' arrangement was wound up in that year.[141] There was also a small-scale recruitment of Italian women for domestic employment, mainly in mental and tuberculosis hospitals and sanatoria in 1950. However, by then the most acute phase of the hospital staffing crisis was over.

If the government's immediate post-war preoccupation had been to meet the needs of hospitals, sanatoria, public institutions and 'hardship' cases, pressure was also mounting from private householders anxious to recruit foreign staff. As early as August 1945 MPs began to demand that 'suitable women from Germany and the European liberated countries' be allowed 'to come under proper supervision to this country', to work as mother's helps.[142] Soon private representations were being made, with influential people contacting the Ministry of Labour to request permission to bring in staff for their own households. In November 1945, for example, Sir Alexander Maxwell, Permanent Under Secretary of State at the Home Office, contacted Sir Godfrey Ince, Permanent Secretary at the Ministry of Labour, to point out that a number of applications had been received by his department asking 'for the admission . . . of aliens to take up domestic employment in private households':

It is represented that the prospective employer is in real need of such help; that domestics are almost impossible to obtain among British subjects, or aliens already here; and that the absence of such help entails real hardship, especially where the prospective employer is elderly or infirm, or has public duties which make it difficult to carry the added burden of domestic work. As instances, I may mention Lady Mary Herbert, one of the Queen's Ladies-in-Waiting, who wishes to obtain a French maid as a personal attendant and to help look after her small girl; and Mr Justice Romer, who asked me the other day if his mother, who is elderly and a cripple, could bring over a Belgian woman to replace her present maid who will shortly be going to Canada with her husband.

We have been obliged to refuse all applications of this kind in order to support the policy of your department where, I understand, the view is taken that if aliens were allowed to come here for domestic employment in private households, the recruitment of foreign women to meet the urgent needs of hospitals and similar institutions would be seriously prejudiced; and that it would be difficult to prevent those already here from drifting into more remunerative and attractive private service.

I find it difficult, however, to give a convincing answer to the applicant who says (as Romer said) - 'Yes, I appreciate that the needs of hospitals must come first; but the woman whom I want to engage has no intention of working in a hospital, and if she can't come to me she won't come at all.'[143]

Violet Markham also joined in the campaign to relax the restrictions, writing to the Ministry of Labour in March 1946: 'I know the difficulties about ministering to the idle rich, but honestly I do not think that a handful of drones ought to stand in the way of alleviating the sufferings and trials of people in a far more modest state of life.[144]

The government, meanwhile, was concerned not only about its hospital recruitment drives, but with the logistics of bringing over large numbers of people from countries whose own transport infrastructure had been shattered and where there was an acute shortage of shipping. However, in April 1946 it agreed that householders who were able to make arrangements with potential foreign domestics could apply to the Ministry of Labour for individual work permits, under terms similar to those which had applied before the war. Initially, preference was to be given to 'hardship' cases, but within months all restrictions had been cast aside.[145]

Immediately there was a great increase in demand, as would-be employers made use of any contacts they had with members of the British Control Commission in Germany, or used the services of private recruitment agencies, or even advertised in the foreign press. During 1946 alone 8,041 domestic permits were issued, 7,622 of them in respect of private residential servants. To get a permit, employers had to satisfy the ministry that the vacancy was 'reasonable and necessary', that they had attempted to get a British worker without success, and that the wages and conditions of employment on offer were, as good as those available to similar British workers in the area. If either party terminated the employment, the foreign domestic must obtain permission from her local employment exchange before taking another post with a different mistress.[146] The work permits were issued for a year initially, but could be extended. They were not granted to women over fifty-five on the grounds that 'the period of full and useful service' they could render was limited and when they reached pensionable age they would 'become chargeable to public funds' if they were unable to work.[147]

Initially, the scheme applied to all nationalities except German women whose presence, so soon after the end of the war, was felt likely to cause discontent among British co-workers.[148] In 1948, however, that changed, partly because of the need to boost the government's recruitment campaign for staff for public institutions and hardship households. From August 1948 an initial group of around two thousand women came in under what was called the North Sea scheme, to cover these official vacancies. At the same time individual German women could be employed by private householders. Soon the burgeoning commercial employment agencies were taking advantage of this new possibility.[149] The Ministry of Labour itself remained studiously aloof from these developments, as an official wrote in December 1948: 'If an employer elects to get in touch with a foreign woman through an employment agency that is his own affair; but the Department does not recognise the agency as having any status in the matter.'[150]

One such agency, Isobel Jay Ltd of Hove, was stressing the benefits of continental recruitment as early as 1949, seeing it as the

> most effective answer to the extreme shortage of domestic labour in this country. . . . In recognition of this need, our OVERSEAS DEPARTMENT has been formed. . . . *More than 2, 000 women and girls* from various European countries . . . have already been placed, and new arrivals

are now landing *almost every day* . . . we have been able to build up such *a well assorted stock if applications*, which we are keeping at such a level as should enable us to nominate potential candidates *for any type of domestic vacancy within a matter of a few days.*[151]

German women and girls were major users of these agencies, with many anxious to escape from the chaos and unemployment in their homeland and also, perhaps, aware that with the enormous loss of men in the Second World War marriage prospects in their own country were relatively slim.[152] As with the refugees who came to Britain before 1939, many of the new, foreign servants had little experience of domestic work and there were complaints in the press and elsewhere that they were taking advantage of the British housewife's need of servants in order to come to Britain for a year to learn the language and to travel around. Agencies were accused of cynically recruiting women with few relevant skills, in order to boost their earnings from booking fees. Some of the girls were of a higher social background than was usual among maids and in the early 1950s Lady Robertson, wife of the British High Commissioner in Germany, commented on this when she met a party of them at a transit camp. 'These fine-looking young ladies do not look like skivvies at all!' she declared in a tactless comment that can have won her few female friends in Britain itself.[153] The *Daily Mail*, in a story headed 'Wunderbar – but can she cook?' was a good deal more critical, observing sourly: 'And when you think of what it cost you to bring her over, and the £3 or so a week you pay her to arrange the flowers and talk broken English, you could kick yourself' for making the appointment.[154]

In some cases the problems were far greater. At Erddig near Wrexham, the eccentric owner, Simon Yorke, engaged three German girls as cheap domestic labour. The house was in an appalling state of repair, with water pouring through the roof into the state rooms when it rained and wet rot rampant. The girls must have been shocked when they arrived, but they clearly resolved to make the best of their situation. Soon they made plans to set up a boarding house in Llandudno, which they partly stocked with items from Erddig. 'Shortly before they left, a procession of carpets and packing cases left the house through the outer stable yard. Subsequently, the shelves for sheets and blankets in the housekeeper's room, neatly labelled in German, were found to be empty.'[155] They had clearly decided to get their own back on their employer.

There were occasional sexual lapses, too, as with a maid from Kassel, recruited by a British doctor and his wife at the end of 1955. She arrived early in February of the following year and three months later gave birth to a child. The employer claimed to have been unaware of the pregnancy because the girl had warned him that she was very stout, nor had it been detected during the medical examination she had undergone before leaving home. She and the baby were returned to Germany a few weeks after the birth.[156]

Overall, during 1949, 8,314 permits were issued to individual German girls to work in Britain. This was more than one in three of all the domestic permits issued in that year (see Table 1). The new Federal German Government, meanwhile, was concerned about the role of the many commercial agencies operating in this field and in late December 1949 an agreement was reached between the British and German authorities designed to bypass them. Under the scheme, British employers could apply for domestic staff to their local employment exchange and, after filling in the relevant forms, these would be sent to a Central Placing Office in Germany. Its task was to match the employer's requirement from its list of German volunteers anxious to take up household work in the United Kingdom. Mistress and maid would then be put in touch with one another and if a satisfactory arrangement were made, the employer would apply for a work permit in the normal way. Once the scheme began in 1950 it was soon followed by an ending of the North Sea recruitment campaign to secure staff for public institutions and hardship households. That was now merged into the new arrangement.[157] From 1950 foreign domestics coming to Britain normally entered either by making individual arrangements with employers or, in the case of German girls, by participation in the Federal Republic's Central Placing organisation. In 1951, a similar central placing plan was applied to Austria.

However, any expectation that these official placements would supersede the role of the commercial agencies was speedily dashed. Even in 1950, under a fifth of the 8,290 German women granted domestic permits came under the Central Placement Scheme. By 1954, when the number of German domestic entrants had fallen to 4,854, under a tenth came under that scheme.[158] The Ministry of Labour in Britain blamed its German counterpart for failing to advertise the plan properly and for creating a situation whereby only about half of British employers applying for staff by this means obtained maids.[159] Yet, it was reluctant to end the arrangement, which limped on into the 1960s.

Already, however, improved conditions in Germany and other European countries meant that by the late 1950s fewer recruits were coming forward. New candidates had to be found, with Spanish and Italian workers becoming more important. By the early 1970s, for example, the then Marquess of Bath depended on a Spanish husband and wife, Michael and Josephine de Soto, to serve as butler-valet and cook. At the beginning of the twentieth century there had been forty-three indoor servants at the marquess's family home at Longleat. Michael, like most butlers at that time, carried out a wide range of duties, including cleaning and doing odd jobs about the house. He also looked after his employer's wardrobe: 'I know when I go to London', declared Lord Bath, 'my clothes are going to be exactly as I want them.'[160]

Not all of the new servants were so successful. Frank Dawes described recently arrived butlers from Spain who turned out to be inexperienced peasants 'dignified with a white jacket'. Already, too, the servant-gathering net had extended into Asia, with 'a vogue for Philippine servants' apparent in the early 1970s.[161] As Table 1 shows, the total of domestic permits granted by the Ministry of Labour remained at a high level to the end of the 1950s, albeit with some increase in the number of workers recruited for schools and other public institutions rather than for private households. It was part of the slow acceptance by some British families that the pre-war world of full-time domestics had gone for ever.

Some wives turned to *au pairs*, a cheaper alternative, whereby in return for a home and pocket money, girls from, in the main, other European countries came to Britain to learn the language and, in return, to take on light household chores and childcare duties. Many of the arrangements worked well. Dr Joyce Chalmers, who was then living in Manchester, remembered that she and her clergyman husband had three *au pairs* from Germany during the mid-to late 1950s. The first was obtained with the help of her mother-in-law, who had earlier been involved in the Control Commission in Germany and who contacted a likely candidate. Ingrid had already spent a year as an *au pair* in Geneva, where she had not been very happy, but she soon settled down in Manchester and remained for over a year. She then recommended the second girl, Edda, who in turn put the family in touch with their third *au pair*, Renate. As Dr Chalmers recalled, the contacts were made purely between the respective families and no official supervision of the girls took place, despite the fact that they were all aged between seventeen and nineteen:

> As for duties we shared the daily routine. Two of the girls enjoyed cooking and quite often produced an excellent meal for us all. We, the *au pair* and myself, shared washing nappies . . . shared washing up . . . and fetching and carrying children and shopping as we had no car. They all went to Manchester 'night school' classes to learn English – and we did our best to ensure that they spoke good English before they left. . . . When, on occasion, I knew I would be unable to share the workload, e.g. when I did a locum for a week or so . . . I employed extra help. . . . I certainly could not have afforded a full-time Nannie, and would have had to depend far more on the good will and kindness of parishioners.[162]

Mrs Helen Hall, another clergy wife in the Manchester area and a friend of Dr Chalmers, recruited two *au pairs* during the 1950s. One was French and the second was German and a cousin of one of her friend's *au pairs*. They, too, attended classes in Manchester and met other class members at the vicarage when they had time off. 'Both came on holiday with us and for them, too, it was a holiday.'[163]

But there was a darker side to the *au pair* picture, with newspapers in France running headlines like: 'In Britain

TABLE 1 *Admission of Individual Foreign Workers under Ministry of Labour Permits: 1946-60*

Year	Total Permits granted (all occupations)	Total Domestic Permits	Total Domestic Permits for Private Service	*Percentage of Total Permits Allocated to Domestic work %*
1946	10,744	8,041	7,622	75
1947	27,002	18,952	17,707	70
1948	28,460	19,395	18,371	68
1949	35,226	23,892	22,556	68
1950	35,035	22,434	20,714	64
1951	36,570	20,474	18,421	56
1952	32,632	18,960	17,014	58
1953	33,832	18,563	16,529	55
1954	36,473	19,043	16,764	52
1955	41,898	21,728	18,614	52
1956	46,117	22,823	n\a	49
1958	42,992	21,138	n\a	49
1958	42,840	20,863	n\a	49
1959	43,371	20,842	n\a	48
1960	50,355	20,969	n\a	42

Private Service as % of Total Domestic Permits

1947	93.4
1948	94.7
1949	94.4
1950	92.3
1951	90.0
1952	89.7
1953	89.0
1954	88.0
1955	85.6

Source: Annual Reports of the Ministry of Labour.

N.B. The workers recruited under this arrangement were additional to those recruited under the official 'Balt Cygnet' and 'Westward Ho' and similar schemes.

2,000 French girls live like slaves.' Even the British press condemned families who exploited their *au pairs* by treating them as cut-price drudges. As E. S. Turner wrote in 1962:

> An *au pair* was supposed to be treated as a member of the family, to accompany them on their social calls, to be given every opportunity to learn the language, and to receive pocket money of between 30s and £2 in return for 'light work'. There were tales of girls forced to do housework or act as nursemaids for twelve hours a day, and to wait at table, or to eat their meals in cafes; there were tales of girls drifting home in a state of dudgeon and, sometimes, in a state of pregnancy; there were also tales of girls who considered themselves above housework of any kind and who arrived with trunks of evening clothes.[164]

There were complaints, too, about the insecurity of the arrangement, with girls sometimes given only a few days notice to leave. They were, therefore, placed in considerable difficulty, unless they had relatives to whom they could turn or were able to get a fresh *au pair* position.[165] The British Government, for its part, refused to take any action to regulate the arrangement by treating the girls as 'employed'. The most it would do was to issue booklets to *au pairs* and their hosts, giving guidance on how to avoid 'misunderstandings and abuse'.[166] It refused all legal responsibility.

In 1964 there were, Celia Briar suggests, around twenty thousand girls coming to work in Britain as *au pairs* through private agencies or informal personal contacts, but in the course of that decade and beyond numbers rose, with many coming to Britain to seek a placement on their own initiative.[167] One estimate in 1993 suggested there were about 170,000 *au pairs* in Britain at that time.[168]

In December 1963, Ministry of Labour figures also suggested around twenty thousand domestic permits were still being issued to foreign servants each year. Around two-thirds of them remained for more than twelve months and most came from western European countries, with Spain, Germany, Italy and Switzerland supplying about two-thirds of the total.[169]

However, not all immigrants wished to take up private, domestic service when they reached the United Kingdom. West Indian women were notable examples of this, although they were prepared to accept cleaning work in hospitals. This they associated with nursing, which they regarded as one of the most desirable professions. When offered private household work, some took the view that this was 'a white woman's job', while most considered they had come to Britain to 'improve' themselves and not to perform menial domestic chores. 'I didn't borrow and save and come all this way just to scrub and clean. I can do that back at home', declared a Jamaican woman on National Assistance, who had refused to take a cleaning job in a café.[170] That was a typical reaction. On the part of employers, too, there is some evidence that racial prejudice played a part in their reluctance to accept West Indian staff and that applied to hospital recruitment in the early 1950s.[171] (See Table 1)

"*Another word of complaint, M'm, and I quits civilian life.*"

1. *Punch* was drawing attention to the difficult mistress-servant relations which manifested themselves in some households at the beginning of the Second World War. (Punch, *13 December 1939*)

"*And now they want another place at table for Henry, Earl of Bolcester, whoever* he *is!*"

2. Footman, with a fashionable striped waistcoat, displaying a less than servile attitude in the seclusion of the kitchen. (Punch, *27 September 1939*)

Above: 4. A London home help cooking in a client's home in March 1953. (*London Metropolitan Photographic Archives*)

Opposite: 3. A batwoman in the WAAF in 1943, relieving the officers in her charge of the 'spit and polish' considered necessary for smartness and efficiency. (*Imperial War Museum Photograph Archives*)

Above: 6. Housework training at the Nottingham centre of the National Institute of Houseworkers in 1949. (*TUC Library*)

Opposite: 5. Hanging up the blackout curtains in September 1939. (*Punch, 27 September 1939*)

Above: 7. Chilton Cantelo House, the first training centre to be opened by the National Institute of Houseworkers. (*Mrs S. Whiting*)

Left: 8. Sheila Chapman in her National Institute of Houseworkers uniform, in training at Chilton Cantelo, August 1949. (*Mrs S. Whiting*)

THE NATIONAL INSTITUTE OF HOUSEWORKERS

DIPLOMA

awarded to

Edith Sheila Chapman

who has satisfied the Board of Examiners
and is admitted an Associate Member of
the National Institute of Houseworkers

Dorothy M. Elliot.   *Chairman*

10th April 1951   *Date*

9. NIH Diploma awarded to Sheila Chapman in 1951. (*Mrs S. Whiting*)

Above: 12. The role of professional cleaning firms is exemplified in this photograph of a *myhome* van delivering clean laundry in 2000. (*myhome*)

Opposite top: 10. Learning to cook at the Oxford centre of the NIH in 1949. (*TUC Library*)

Opposite bottom: 11. Students making pickles and chutney at the Bridge of Allan training centre in Scotland in 1948. (*TUC Library*)

MRS. HUNT'S AGENCY

ESTABLISHED 1898

TELEPHONE: 020 7229 3506   9.30 TO 5.30 Mon – Fri.

NO ENGAGEMENT, NO FEE

PERMANENT STAFF

Living-out Staff:
FIRST-CLASS CLEANERS WHO ALSO IRON, COMPANIONS,
HOUSEKEEPERS, COOKS etc.

We charge a one-off agency introduction fee of:
Four times the weekly wage for Cleaners, Mothers' Helps,
Housekeepers, Cooks etc.
The employee is paid and employed by the Client.

TRIAL PERIOD for all categories of living-out staff:
If the employee leaves within eight weeks of the engagement or if the
employee proves to be unsuitable during this trial period, we will
make a discretionary replacement on condition that our invoice has
been paid by the settlement date as stated on the invoice.

Living-in Staff:
Carers, Companions, Mothers' Helps, Housekeepers,
Cooks and all staff who live-in:

**We charge the Client a fee of eight times the net weekly wage for jobs
within the UK.**

We have supplied the best staff for over 100 years.
All staff are interviewed & have excellent suitable references which we verify.

Please read all four sides of the terms and conditions, which are contractually
binding.

Above: 13. Domestic agencies, like the long-established Mrs. Hunt's Agency, played an important role in providing household staff, especially in the larger towns and cities. Mrs. Hunt's took great care to ensure that all their foreign domestics had the appropriate legal status, to protect their many 'high profile' customers. (*William Weber, Mrs Hunt's Agency*)

Opposite top: 14. A London home help arranging flowers for an elderly client in 1963. Such helpers provided social contact as well as domestic assistance for invalids and those unable to get about easily. (*London Metropolitan Photographic Archives*)

Opposite bottom: 15. Professional cleaning services provided by *myhome* in 2000. Staff were carefully vetted and fully experienced. To achieve maximum efficiency cleaners worked in teams of two, with the back-up of a supervisor. (*myhome*)

Above: 16. An old-style 'daily' cleaning the steps at a London public house in 1962. Her shoulders had become hunched by long years of hard work. (*London Metropolitan Photographic Archives*)

Left: 17. After 1945 attempts were made to attract young people into the hotel and catering industry, by the issue of such publications as *Personal Service: Careers for Boys and Girls in the Catering Industry* (1946), from which this illustration is taken. (*TUC Library*)

18. Arthur R. Inch, employed as a single-handed butler, around the time he retired from the Kleinwort family's service in 1980. (*Arthur R. Inch*)

Left: 19. Training to be a chef on a catering course at the South-East London Technical College, Lewisham Way, in 1973. (*London Metropolitan Photographic Archives*)

Below: 20. The skills of waiting at table being learnt on a catering course at the South-East London Technical College in 1973. (*London Metropolitan Photographic Archives*)

Part two

The Final Decades

Domestic help is now as large an industry in the UK as it was just before the Second World War. . . . Many people with a career and a fair amount of disposable income require, and possess the means to buy in, assistance with cleaning, laundry and even cooking, when necessary. Large numbers of working couples and single parents have to have someone to look after their children on a regular basis. Elderly people are also employing more domestic help, either because they need support in the home or simply to free up more leisure time.

Lynn Brittney, *The Which? Guide to Domestic Help* (London, 1998), p. 9.

THE DOMESTIC SCENE

During the final decades of the twentieth century there was a noticeable revival in paid domestic work, after the years of decline followed by modest resurgence, which had characterised the period from 1939 to the early 1960s. In 1996 the *Economist* announced that 'Britain [had] rediscovered servants'. In evidence it pointed out that whereas in 1985 the nation had spent the equivalent of £1.45 billion on all kinds of home help, by 1995 that had more than doubled to £3.89 billion. As a share of total household expenditure, domestic service had risen from 0.4 per cent at the earlier date to 0.9 per cent.[1] Later research suggests that this upward trend continued.[2] Hence the *Economist's* assertion that between the mid-1980s and the mid-1990s domestic service was the most rapidly expanding area of consumer spending. A contributor to *The Times* in September 1998 agreed, calling it 'Britain's biggest growth industry'.[3]

Yet that did not mean a return to the starchy Edwardian world of upstairs-downstairs, with retinues of uniformed housemaids, parlourmaids, cooks, general servants, butlers and footmen conferring status on the households they served as well as carrying out domestic duties. As in the post-war period, there was a careful avoidance of the words 'maid' or 'servant' in advertisements for staff. Instead of general servants, mother's helps or housekeepers were sought, while nursemaids were transformed into 'nannies'. The new labour force was expected to be more flexible and, in the main, less formal than its pre-1939 predecessor. Its role was generally functional rather than ceremonial. Although multi-staff households survived and still employed a few thousand workers, only a wealthy minority recruited the full panoply of butler, cook, housekeeper, full-time gardener and chauffeur. Even these households were likely to rely on married couples to supply their resident domestic help, with the man taking on the duties of butler or gardener-cum-chauffeur and his wife those of cook-housekeeper. Additional assistance was provided by 'dailies' or by contract workers hired for special occasions. New categories of free-lance service providers emerged to meet the needs of the burgeoning 'cash rich, time poor' dual income households of the professional middle classes. Among these were dog walkers and flower arrangers, as well as outside caterers brought in to prepare special dinner parties or buffet suppers and suppliers of laundry services whose professionalism contrasted markedly with the old-style weekly washerwoman.[4]

In this new world, efforts were made to create a spirit of egalitarianism between employer and worker, but these attempts to reduce class barriers did not prevent cleaning, in particular, from being regarded as a low status occupation. Interestingly, domestic work in private households was explicitly excluded from the protection of the 1974 Health and Safety at Work Act because of the practical problems of enforcement and the invasion of privacy which would have occurred if inspectors had been empowered to enter such households.

One girl, who had formerly been a student, expressed resentment that as a cleaner she was 'looked down upon. People . . . ask me when I am going to do something "proper". I feel quite incensed because somebody has to do cleaning. Why have the attitude that only lesser people can do it?'[5] Another woman, who had set up her own cleaning business when she found office work too monotonous, agreed. 'The people who look down on you tend to be the ones who don't have a lot of money. They are never satisfied and expect you to spring-clean the whole house in just a few hours.'[6]

Even in July 2000, the historian and media personality, David Starkey, could equate domestic service with 'relatively low-level employment', adding: 'It's ridiculous that people at the top are killing themselves in demanding jobs and then coming home to mow their own lawns.'[7]

Although it was widely agreed that a strong revival in paid household work had occurred, the precise numbers of those involved proved difficult to estimate. This was partly because recent population censuses and government employment statistics had stopped covering these sectors of the labour force in detail and partly because it could be attributed to the large amount of 'informal' work that took place. This affected cleaners, in particular and they comprised the largest single category in the new labour force. Many, as part-timers, did not declare an income. Some wanted to be paid 'cash-in-hand' because they were supplementing a state benefit received by themselves or their partner; others might be seeking extra income to boost earnings from another job. That applied to Sharon, who had three children and was married to a milkman. She got into private domestic cleaning initially because she was approached by a potential employer while she was working in a school canteen. After the birth of her third child she gave up the school job and continued with her private work. At that stage domestic cleaning afforded her an opportunity to supplement household income while continuing to be a full-time mother, since she was able to take her youngest child with her when she went to work.[9]

In some cases, especially around London, these 'informal' cleaners included foreigners whose lack of a work permit and uncertain residential status precluded recruitment into the formal labour market.[10] Such women were vulnerable to exploitation by householders – and agencies – who might take advantage of their illegal status. However, after the passage of the 1996 Asylum and Immigration Act, employers could face prosecution and a fine of up to £5,000 per worker if they knowingly took on, or offered work to, a person who did not have a right to work in the United Kingdom.[11] Yet that did not prevent the less scrupulous from hiring this cheap, compliant labour. Even the introduction in April 1999 of the National Minimum Wage of £3.60 an hour for adults and £3 for those aged eighteen to twenty-one is unlikely to benefit such people, because of their lack of legal standing and consequent bargaining power.[12]

The rise in demand for domestic staff, particularly in the 1980s and 1990s, was attributable to four main factors. The first was the growing polarity of incomes between rich and poor which manifested itself especially in London and the south-east of England, the areas where the pressure for domestic recruitment was greatest. In Britain the real disposable incomes of the wealthiest 10 per cent of the population rose by an estimated 62 per cent between 1979 and 1991, while those of the poorest 10 per cent fell by 17 per cent over the same period. In London that polarisation was most obvious with one commentator claiming that during the 1980s the difference between the earnings of those on the highest and the lowest incomes was twice as large in the capital as in the rest of the country.[13] Part of the increasing disparity could be linked to the high salaries that the top earners could command, particularly in the City of London, but it was affected, too, by the reduced tax burden on the wealthy and by the growing benefit dependency of the poorest families as a result of unemployment, single parenthood or invalidity. High unemployment meant that even some of those who stayed in work had to 'trade down' and take less skilled and less remunerative posts when they were made redundant. The outcome was that not only could wealthier householders afford domestic help, but some of the worst off (especially women) wanted to earn cash 'on the side' to supplement their incomes. Casual cleaning was particularly useful in this regard. It was easy to take up, since most employers believed that all women were capable of carrying it out and so they had no need to test competency, and it was inconspicuous. For householders the main concern was that new recruits should be honest, reliable and punctual.

A second factor encouraging the rise in domestic staff and one associated with the first point was the increase in the number of two-income families. Women became an increasingly important part of the labour force, with almost three-quarters of those of working age in paid work in 1997, compared to under three-fifths in 1971.[14] Many at the upper end of the salary scale were holding demanding professional and managerial postions which required long working hours and a good deal of personal commitment. Despite feminist pressure for greater equality between male and female partners in carrying out household chores and despite the proliferation of labour-saving appliances designed to cut down manual tasks, much time-consuming domestic work remained the responsibility of women, ranging from ironing clothes to dusting and polishing the furniture. Hiring a cleaner, while reinforcing the gender divisions within the home was one way in which a woman could avoid the stress of juggling the demands of household and workplace. At the same time she was 'buying' leisure, in that her weekends and other free time no longer had to be devoted to household chores.

In a survey of high-earning working couples in London and in the south-east and the north-east of England, Nicky Gregson and Michelle Lowe discovered during the 1980s that over a third employed domestic waged labour irrespective of geography.[15] That meant, of course, that around two-thirds did not. In those cases, Gregson and

Lowe concluded, there was either a greater willingness by the male partner to share the chores, or the female partner was anxious to demonstrate that she was a 'proper' wife by taking on traditional household tasks in the way her mother had perhaps done.[16] This was true of the Collins family. Pauline Collins was a medical researcher and her husband was an investment banker. Until their first child was born they employed no domestic labour. Neither Pauline's mother nor her mother-in-law had been in paid employment and they had always done their own housework, as had Pauline herself prior to her marriage at the age of thirty-two. When she married she had been 'very keen to be a proper wife'. She had wanted to show her husband, her family, her in-laws and herself that she was able to combine a successful career with the duties of a housewife. Only when children arrived was that no longer feasible and she then recruited a nanny and a cleaner.[17]

Pauline Collins's dilemma was shared by other highly paid women who continued to work after having a baby. Kay, a psychologist and mother of four, who had been brought up with the egalitarian ideals of the 1950s and 1960s, felt uncomfortable about taking on domestic help when her first baby arrived. 'I had decided I could not cope with employing another woman because of the status thing, but I found two salt-of-the-earth types who seemed to get real pleasure out of cleaning. But I was always very apologetic and used to give them extra money from time to time because I felt guilty.'[18]

Significantly, in 1998 it was estimated that half of all women with children under ten years were in paid employment.[19] That inevitably meant a high demand for childcare facilities. While some mothers found these in the form of childminders, nursery schools and through the help of family and friends, for a substantial minority, nannies were the solution. They were, in some respects, a product of the post-war view in Britain that motherhood was not only a full-time occupation, but it was home-based. Parents who were anxious that their child should spend his or her earliest pre-school years in the security of the home, or those who had several young children to be cared for, were particularly likely to find nannies attractive. In such situations, a nanny was far more flexible and probably cheaper than the alternative forms of childcare. Another possibility was to share the nanny's services with a neighbour, thereby dividing the cost as well. As a result, nannies became second only to cleaners as a rapidly expanding sector of the 'new' domestic economy. They might be resident or non-resident, but were often in sole charge of the household during the day. When employers' marriages broke up or there were serious family difficulties, the nanny might be the only stable influence in the children's lives. The number of nannies employed is hard to quantify. Estimates made in 1996-7 ranged between 100,000 and 200,000. Again, the fact that some women were employed under casual 'cash-in-hand' conditions meant that they were not entered in any official records.[20]

A fourth cause of the increased demand for help (and one largely ignored by writers like Gregson and Lowe) arose from the greater number of old people in the population. In the mid-1980s this contributed to an increase in the number of local authority home helps, but in the 1990s budgetary pressures and changes in government policy meant a reduction in the supply of such helpers (who, in any case, were now expected to take on more nursing duties and less domestic work). The charges levied for their services also increased in many areas. Nevertheless, in the mid-1990s around 8 per cent of people over the age of sixty-five were being assisted by local authority home helps, and a further 7 per cent were using the services of private helpers. This latter proportion had increased from 4 per cent reporting the use of private helps in 1991-2. Among those aged seventy-five or above, 15 per cent had local authority help and 11 per cent relied on private provision in the mid-1990s. In other words, among the oldest group of pensioners more than a quarter depended on some form of home help.[21] In addition, the increased number of nursing homes and residential care facilities catering for the elderly had their own domestic help requirements, which added to the general level of demand from this sector.

Some domestic cleaning businesses, like Gene Riley's Help Unlimited, set up in Loughborough in the mid-1980s, concentrated on providing for the elderly or for invalids. Gene set up her firm when serious illness forced her to stop teaching and, for a time, she had to rely on the aid of friends and neighbours: 'It occurred to me that there must be a hell of a lot of people who can't. . . . There is a thin line between caring and cleaning that's to do with well-being.' It was that need her business was designed to satisfy.[22]

For older people who were housebound or who had few relatives living locally, these services were often an important source of companionship as well as domestic assistance. Mrs Sheila Whiting, who became a home help in Cornwall in the early 1960s and continued in the post for over twenty-six years, welcomed the work, not only because it fitted in with her own domestic responsibilities, but because it enabled her to meet a variety of people. Among many elderly clients she discovered that a well-scrubbed front doorstep 'was their pride and joy'. Other tasks she carried out included blackleading grates, washing and lighting fires: 'one dear old soul never had any sticks so we would make newspaper curls . . . many confided in you with family problems, close secrets, but it must have been very hard for them to lose their independence and rely on others to do their work. . . . I have always enjoyed cleaning, cooking; it gives great satisfaction to the mind.'[23]

Other home helps found the tight schedule they had to maintain in visiting clients and the hardships they witnessed among poorer pensioners too stressful and gave up the work. That applied to Annie Spike, who was employed in Hackney.

> Home-help work is a very depressing job . . . I was getting too involved in it. . . . I went to . . . people who used to count the pieces of coal they put on the fire, because they were frightened they wouldn't have enough later . . . I used to visit about five old people a day, from 10 till 2 – and I was timed on each person. They expected a terrible lot from you . . . I had to walk from one to the other.[24]

After a few months she left and took a job in a shop. Later she became an office cleaner, working two hours each evening. 'Some women go into office cleaning to get away from the house', she declared, 'for a change of atmosphere from their worries and problems, not so much for the money.'[25]

If householders wished to recruit their staff independently, rather than relying on local authority home helps, they had four main options open to them. The first and the best was to utilise personal contacts and individual recommendations. In London, where there were numerous immigrant workers, ethnic networks might provide a candidate. 'Employers find a cleaner by asking neighbours, who will then talk to their cleaners and cleaners will pass employers on to relatives or friends who need work. In this way jobs tend to stay concentrated within a particular ethnic community.'[26] In the capital women from Portugal, Spain and the Philippines were widely thought to be better workers than their British counterparts and to display a more suitably subservient attitude.

When these methods failed, the second choice was to advertise, perhaps locally in a newspaper or even in a shop window, when a cleaner was required. For specialist staff like nannies, butlers and cooks, prestigious national newspapers and magazines like *The Lady* would be selected. *The Lady*, which has been dubbed the *Exchange and Mart* of domestic help in modern Britain, normally included around 300 advertisements each week. From 1997 it also ran a 'Nanny of the Year' award offering £1,000 and other benefits to the successful candidate and encouraging satisfied employers to nominate their own nanny for consideration.[27]

The advertisements revealed employers' priorities and expectations as well as the vacancies available. Among those seeking nannies, it was more common to mention that applicants must be non-smokers or able to drive a car than that they should possess formal qualifications – although that might be raised at an interview. (The first official qualification for nannies had been established in 1945 with the formation of the National Nursery Board or NNEB.) In some cases, multiple duties might be proposed. Thus of seventy-six advertisements for nannies in *The Lady* during the week 20-26 June 2000, eighteen required cleaning or other household tasks as well. Thirty specified the nanny must be a non-smoker; and twenty-six that she be able to drive a car; just five stated that she must be qualified. Typical of many was an appeal for a resident

> Nanny/Housekeeper, Clapham. Mid-July or September. Informal professional family. Sole charge charming schoolboy (6) Monday-Friday plus some housework, laundry and cooking. Experienced non-smoker with excellent references. Must be well organised, reliable, cheerful and flexible.

Then there was an advertisement for a Mother's Help/Nanny/Housekeeper inserted by a 'family with 2 boys, 3 and 5 and a dog in Regent's Park. Live-in, non-smoking person to do housework, childcare and cooking.

A third possibility, and one particularly useful when there was an urgent vacancy to fill, was to apply to an agency. Many had grown up in the final quarter of the century to match the rise in demand for household help. Their main merits were that they were likely to have people on their books who were available immediately and whom they could send for interview. They could be valuable, too, in supplying temporary staff. William Weber, partner in the long-established Mrs Hunt's Agency in London, noted that June and July were particularly busy for his firm because the season was 'in full swing and customers all require extra staff for their parties and the school holidays'.[28] When engaging permanent workers, his clients demanded someone with diverse skills. 'Someone who can cook, book an airline ticket, dash down to Ludgrove to pick up little Johnny, take the dog to the vet – they want someone just like them.' Yet that did not mean that staff of roughly the same social status as their employers were treated as equals. One helper long remembered the snub administered by a woman whose house she was cleaning. The mistress walked up to her and wiped the lipstick from her face, saying cuttingly at the same time: 'Did you think you had come for a cocktail party?' At the end of the century the bulk of the firm's work was 'in placing dailies (or twice weeklies) who will clean and iron'. They, and the mother's helps, were normally paid £7 per hour, plus their bus fares. Most applicants came from overseas, particularly from Spain, Portugal, Poland and the Philippines.[29]

Agencies, especially in London, could be expensive for employers. In addition to initial registration charges of £15 to £30, several hundred pounds might be required for the successful placing of senior staff in prestigious locations. Even temporary placements might cost between £55 and £500.[30] Employers anxious to ensure they were using reputable firms could obtain a list of approved businesses from the Federation of Employment and Recruitment Agencies, which could be supplemented by information in the Department of Education and Employment's booklet, *Need a Nanny?*

published in 1999 and by its Childcare Link, which could be contacted by telephone.[31]

Another option was to apply to a training school, especially when specialist staff like nannies, chefs or butlers were required. However, apart from the fact that new graduates were likely to be inexperienced, in the case of prestigious establishments like Norland College, they could prove expensive and highly competitive as well, with several families trying to recruit the same candidate. In other cases, as with Ivor Spencer's International School for Butler Administrators, Personal Assistants and Estate Managers (established in 1981) there might be strong foreign competition.[32] A well-trained, unflappable English butler or a British nanny could be a status symbol for employers overseas as well as in the United Kingdom. As Rosie Cox points out, the 'largest training centre in London' had its own placement agency in the United States.[33] As before the Second World War, there was a steady trickle of senior British-born servants who wished to work abroad.

All this forced up staff salaries and the best qualified workers expected good living accommodation, the use of a car and liberal holidays as well. On the other hand, for those lower down the scale or working outside London, the position was very different, with long hours and relatively poor pay the order of the day. The position of nannies might be affected, too, by the fact that when warm relations developed between them and their charges (what

Gregson and Lowe label feelings of 'false kinship'), they might be reluctant to pressurise employers over pay. One girl realised after she had been in her post for about six months that the family for whom she was working was in financial difficulties. She knew that her salary was due to be reviewed shortly but 'I thought, I can't say anything . . . I'm so happy that I would rather not mention it and stay. . . .' She kept silent and was eventually given a £20-a-week rise by the employers. However, months later she was still uncertain about what would happen when the next pay review became due. 'I'm not going to say anything. I'm just going to wait for them to say it' [34]

Gregson and Lowe's researches revealed that of twenty-five nannies that they interviewed in the north-east of England during the 1980s, none had take-home pay above £120 a week and over half received between £65 and £80 a week net. By contrast, of twenty-five girls interviewed in the south-east, the highest paid received more than £160 a week and under a quarter obtained less than £100 a week.[35] A fully trained Norland nurse at the end of the 1990s could cost as much as £400 a week, with national insurance contributions to be added on top.[36]

For those seeking cleaners, one possibility was to avoid personal recruitment altogether by going to one of the home cleaning firms which had sprung up in the 1980s and 1990s. These ranged from small enterprises set up by a single person working with a small staff on a very local basis to major businesses like Molly Maids UK, one of Britain's biggest domestic cleaning companies. Their chief executive noted that the kind of client the firm was getting had changed considerably in the late 1990s. 'More than half are young professionals, couples or just flatmates who don't want to spend the whole weekend arguing about whose turn it is to clean the bathroom. . . . We are talking about people who have never had a cleaning lady in their family before.'[37]

Another of these large-scale enterprises, set up early in 2000, was *myhome*, a subsidiary of Unilever. It offered a high-quality laundry service, home cleaning and the hire of linen. Initially its operations were concentrated in south west London, but there were plans for it to expand across the country.[38]

These home cleaning businesses were normally more expensive than a personally recruited 'daily', but for those able to afford it, the service had several advantages. They included a greater opportunity to arrange times and work schedules which suited the householder, the carrying out of work to a high standard by vetted staff and anonymity. With this method, employers might never meet their cleaners. That appealed to those anxious to avoid the intimacy of face-to-face contacts with a regular cleaner, or who felt guilty because they were not carrying out their own chores. Such commercial alternatives resembled the purchase of other household services, like painting and decorating or dry cleaning.

Anne-Marie Daly, a trainee solicitor in her early thirties, was one young professional who chose to employ a daily cleaner, but in her case it was a local pensioner rather than an agency that performed the service. Despite its greater cheapness, it had its downside. 'She talks constantly and occasionally breaks things, but I don't like to mention it in case she leaves. . . . There's a fine line between being friendly and too friendly. I've found the best way of doing things is to go out and leave her a note . . . she knows she can always help herself to drink.'[39] In the late 1990s, Daly, who lived in Cheshire, paid her cleaner £4.50 an hour and admitted that she had poached her from a neighbour. 'I heard on the grapevine that she was being paid £3 an hour and had to work hard for that, so I rang her up and offered more. Her old boss was furious but I didn't feel guilty about it.' In London and Bath, however, some cleaners charged as much as £9 an hour.

From the worker's point of view, being recruited by a home cleaning firm had the advantage of agreed working conditions and wages, without the need to negotiate with individual employers. Relations with householders could be businesslike, without the need for subservience. There was also less opportunity for employers to show arrogance or unreasonable behaviour. Even a householder like Jane Shilling, who referred to the supervisor of the team of young women who had taken over her domestic chores as the Obergruppenführer, kept in the background if she was at home when they arrived.[40]

However, experienced cleaners, working on a free-lance basis in areas where the demand for staff was high, were also able to lay down their conditions. Yvonne, who was in her mid-thirties and had been cleaning for twelve years, had ten different employers in the late 1990s, going to two each weekday. She had a waiting list for her services as well:

> I don't do ironing because I hate it and I won't clean ovens, it would take too much time out of my three-hour stretch and the house wouldn't be done properly. All my ladies are very nice and don't treat me like a servant – I wouldn't stay if they did. I worked for a woman once who used to sprinkle peanuts in corners to make sure I was using the vacuum properly. She also insisted I call her Mrs Bennett, which I don't mind if ladies are elderly but she was only a few years older than me. I only stayed a month. So many women work these days that they need me more than I need them.[41]

While warm feelings could exist between nannies and their employers, there was always the potential for tension and disagreements. Sue Richney, in her early twenties, had been a nanny since the age of sixteen. She had been in her current post eighteen months when she was interviewed early in 2000. As a resident worker she experienced enforced intimacy with her employers, since unlike the situation before 1939, there were no longer strict social demarcations between employer and employee, with each 'knowing her place'. This made for difficulties. 'You are with them every day', declared Sue. 'You witness their personal lives at first hand. . . . If there's a family feud going on for example, you just get out of the room and find yourself something to do. You know it's none of your business. . . . It's a very personal, close relationship. . . . But at the same time you have to keep a professional distance.'[42]

Kay Crosse, the principal of Norland College, agreed, emphasising the need for staff to maintain confidentiality and discretion. 'A nanny not only has to be equipped to look after the children, she also needs . . . social skills to negotiate the tensions and complexities of family life. . . . It's hard to maintain the purely employer-employee relationship when you're sharing the intimacy of a family home.' For this reason many nannies preferred to live out, since this gave them freedom to develop their own interests and friendships outside working hours.

Further problems arose when working mothers felt guilty because they were not looking after their child themselves in a way that conformed to social expectations, even at the end of the twentieth century. One woman, whose two-year-old son was cared for by a nanny on three days a week, called it a 'doomed relationship', leading to inner turmoil and even competition for the child's love and attention:

I think my nanny's really good . . . and I'd recommend her to anyone, but I hate her. Everything about her irritates me. . . . You desperately want your nanny to love your child because you want her to protect the child as if it was her own. You want your child to feel completely secure within a relationship of intimacy and love, but at the same time that excludes you. . . . They know if you sack them you endanger your child's emotional health, plus you have the whole rigmarole of going to an agency, paying out lots of money to find a new nanny who probably won't please you any more than the last.[43]

Other mothers told of 'worrying incidents', like the Swedish nanny who ran a flourishing drugs business from her bedroom and the disgruntled girl who put a brick through her employers' window.[44] These anxieties became more acute when occasional tragic incidents of serious child abuse occurred, as in the case of a young Australian nanny who was found guilty early in 1999 of killing the baby in her care by violent shaking.[45] There were sensational reports in the press which gave the impression that such misconduct was commonplace rather than a rarity. Journalists hastened to describe their own experience in highly coloured language. One contributor to the *Guardian*, in an article headed, 'We must do better than this. Another nanny scandal, another child dead', complained of the lack of formal standards against which parents could measure the nannies who came for interview:

The reason I've become quite good at making accurate character assessments over a cup of coffee, is that in the past I have made so many inaccurate ones. I once hired a nanny who fed my toddler Aspirins by the bottle. I hired another who dropped him on his head *while I was sitting in the next room*. Another had a violent boyfriend. A few others were pathological liars. And even the very best were sometimes really too young to cope with the pressures that came with being 'part of the family', in a job that wasn't really a job.[46]

Her solution was for families who hired nannies to be given tax breaks to enable them to pay higher salaries and for there to be better training. This would mean that 'people would go into childcare work because they were good at it, and not as a last resort'.

It was partly in response to the moral panic aroused by the sad case of the Australian nanny that the government issued its *Need a Nanny?* guide in 1999. A year later it required all agencies dealing with nannies to check the background and qualifications of applicants before passing them on to potential employers.[47] But since under a third of nannies were hired through agencies, with the rest being recruited by advertisements or personal contacts, this still left loopholes which let cruel or inadequate workers slip through the net. Hence the emphasis in the *Need a Nanny?* booklet that it was the parents' responsibility to make sure that they obtained the right person. 'There are no legal requirements on a person applying to work as a nanny. . . . *Remember, it is your responsibility as the employer to ensure that you are completely satisfied with the person that you employ.*'[48]

As in earlier years, many less affluent employers turned to the cheaper alternatives of mother's helps or *au pairs* for their childcare needs. Few of these were likely to have qualifications, although mother's helps might be experienced. *Au pairs* were unlikely to have much knowledge of how to look after children and were considered unsuitable to care for pre-school youngsters whose parents were at work. However, some parents did take that risk. Their conditions were regulated by the Home Office and until May 1998 they had to register with the police. After that date only the nationals of a very few countries were still required to register; of these, Turkey was the most important.[49] They had to be single, aged between seventeen and twenty-seven when first entering the country and were to remain for a maximum of two years. No girl (or from the mid-1990s, boy) was allowed to take employment in the United Kingdom, the light household duties which were part of the *au pair* arrangement being deemed merely recompense for the hospitality afforded by the hostess. He or she was limited to five hours' household duties a day and was to have two free days each week. The intention was that *au pairs* should learn something of the language and culture of Britain while they lived in the country, rather than just

be cheap servants. In return for their duties, they were
to receive pocket money of around £35 to £40 a week.
After the UK's entry into the European Union in the early
1970s, in strictly legal terms they were to come only from
a short list of non-EU countries, since citizens of the EU
were free to live and work anywhere within its borders.
At the end of the 1990s *au pairs* were defined as nationals
of certain eastern European countries, such as Croatia,
the Czech Republic, Hungary, the Slovak Republic and
Slovenia, as well as a limited number of other places,
including Cyprus, Malta, Switzerland and Turkey.[50] Total
numbers allowed in varied from month to month. In July
1998, 1,680 entered the United Kingdom, of whom 680
came from Slovakia and 610 from the Czech Republic; in
November 1998, there were 870 entrants, with the Czech
Republic providing 360 and Slovakia 190. Turkey came
third, with 120 *au pairs*.[51]

In 1999, there were estimated to be around 25,000
au pairs in the country under these arrangements, but
in reality that was a gross under-estimate. As in earlier
years, the vast majority of *au pair* positions were filled by
youngsters coming from such European Union countries
as France, Spain, Italy and Germany.[52] There were also
illegal entrants from other countries such as Poland.[53]
One estimate in 1993 put the true total of *au pairs* in
Britain as close to 170,000.[54]

Many *au pairs* also operated outside the regulations.
Some because they worked longer hours than laid down,

in a capacity described as '*au pair* plus'; others because they were not studying English; and others again because, like the Polish girls, they came from non-participating countries. They might also perform tasks that were outside the 'light housework' category. Adele, a young German girl who came to Britain in April 1969, obtained her first placement in Feltham after scanning a wide range of advertisements in the London *Evening Standard*. Her duties involved dressing and taking a six-year-old boy to school, collecting him in the late afternoon and in the evening bathing and feeding him and putting him to bed. She also carried out various household chores, but normally had the evenings free after about 7 p.m. She had a day off on Sunday. In addition, however, she did a good deal of driving around in the family car. That included taking a piece of machinery from her host's ice cream business to be repaired in Colchester. Relations between family and *au pair* remained good until she had two accidents with the car within a few days of one another. After the second she virtually gave up driving and her weekly pocket money was docked by her hosts to help cover the cost of repairs. She now had to take the little boy to school by train and the underground, rather than by car, and that added to strained feelings within the household. Eventually, in July, the hostess said that Adele was not carrying out her domestic tasks properly. She suggested that the girl should leave within a few days. The charge was later withdrawn, but Adele, resenting the reproofs and feeling that it was the family who had made the rooms untidy, decided to go anyway. She went to stay with her married sister, who lived in Surbiton, for a short time.

Soon other *au pair* placements followed, including one lasting about two or three weeks when she became a receptionist at a hotel in South Kensington, with the hotel manager acting as her 'host'. She was provided with a small room on the premises, but had the galling experience of having her slender cash reserves stolen. Not until January 1970 did she finally obtain a settled position as an *au pair* with an American free-lance photographer and her daughter. As Adele confided to her friend in Germany, she had at last found a pleasant family where she was well treated. Although she did not enjoy housework, overall the placement was first rate (*ganz prima*). Throughout this whole unsettled period she attended her English classes conscientiously and succeeded in passing her examinations. She also enjoyed a hectic social life in her free time.[55]

Rather like mistresses discussing incompetent maids in Victorian times, many hosts and hostesses of *au pairs* had their 'horror' stories. Maureen Lipman described how one girl 'borrowed' her best silk suit and returned with it 'scrunched up in a bag between mud-covered boots and a Braun Ladyshave. . . . There comes a time in every *au pair* employer's life when another three weeks of saying "Zis is ze washing machine" . . . is anathema. At such moments, the urge to buy British is very strong.'[56] Similarly, Martin Plimmer in *The Times* compared his cheerful Spanish *au pair* to a 'euphoric Great Dane. . . . Everything makes her laugh: children, pets, the washing machine. . . . I can't shout at her though: this is a girl who, in her spare time, helps out at a centre for Guatemalan orphans. . . . Other *au pairs* I have disliked with a free conscience. Not Belen. Even as I list these resentments, I picture her playing her trumpet to Guatemalan urchins and I feel ashamed. I cannot sack her.'[57]

However, for many families the attraction of *au pairs* was not their character but their cheapness. When in 1999 it was proposed to bring them within the provisions of the National Minimum Wage there was an immediate outcry from parents, as well as in the Press and in Parliament. In January of that year a contributor to *The Times* predicted such a move would herald the end of the *au pair* system, since working families of modest means would not be able to afford them. A couple who employed a Turkish girl admitted that they could easily pay higher wages, but argued that this 'would break the bond of trust that [existed] between them and their *au pair*'. The husband claimed that as employers they would 'probably be much more demanding, making sure that things like the ironing [were] properly done'.[58] In the end the protests succeeded. The new regulations exempted people working and living as part of a family in the way that *au pairs* did. They were to continue to receive their

£40 or so per week pocket money, plus free board and lodging.[59]

A variation on the theme was the 'Working Holidaymakers' arrangement, whereby girls aged from seventeen to twenty-seven who came from Commonwealth countries could enter Britain to work either part-time for two years (that is, up to twenty-five hours per week), or full-time for one year. Many women from Australia, New Zealand and Canada took domestic posts in this way, since these usually provided them with a home as well as a small income. One such girl was Joanne, who came to Britain from Australia. She was a fully trained nanny and decided to become a 'holiday nanny', looking after the families of British expatriates who had returned to Britain for a short time. She worked for up to a month at a stretch, until her employers either returned to their posting or took up a fresh position and all of her jobs were residential.[60]

Immigrant domestics, too, played a significant role in many households and, in general, they worked on a longer-term basis than *au pairs* and 'working holidaymakers'. That was true in the 1970s when, despite a general tightening of the work permit scheme, the need for domestic staff in homes, hospitals and hotels led to the provision of special quotas for foreign servants, of whom an increasing number came from the Philippines, Spain and Portugal. Later, when Spain and Portugal joined the European Union in 1986, their citizens were free to travel without permits. They came because pay and conditions were better than they could secure in their homeland. As Rosie Cox points out, British householders welcomed them, often in preference to local employees. Portuguese women were particularly sought after as housekeepers, while Filipinos knew 'how to clean everything properly. . . . And you should see their ironing! . . . English women just can't do that, they don't do it right.'[61]

Between 1973 and 1976, 7,278 permits were issued to entrants from the Philippines alone, mainly for domestic purposes. Indeed, in 1975, two-thirds of permits issued to resident domestics were allocated to Filipinos.[62] However, over the course of the 1970s the quotas were progressively reduced and from August 1977 only European women were allowed to enter Britain as domestic workers. At the end of 1979, the quota system was ended altogether. From 1980, as a special concession, foreigners visiting or settling in Britain were allowed to bring their domestic servants with them, as were returning British expatriates. Permits were awarded in respect of the servants for a year at a time and during the first four years of their stay workers were not allowed to leave their posts. Indeed, their passports were stamped 'employment prohibited' and a note was added that they were accompanyirig a particular employer. Only after four years could they apply to settle in Britain long term and, if permission were granted, they might then change their employer as well. During those first four years they endured what has been described as virtual slavery. Many suffered physical or sexual ill-treatment, while others lived in poor accommodation or were unable to obtain their wages and had their passports withheld. One victim was Sally, a Filipina, who worked for a family from Dubai. Once they reached London, Sally's already miserable existence worsened. 'They hold my passport and they lock me in all the time. . . . And here I have to sleep on the floor of the toilet where the children trample over me.' Her work was harder, too. 'They say everything in London very expensive so I must wash the sheets, clean the windows three floors up.' She received no wages and was told she would only be paid when the family returned to Abu Dhabi. After enduring this mistreatment for four months, she decided to escape. She crawled out of a third floor window, but in the process fell to the ground, breaking her pelvis and arm. She was in hospital for two months and during that time was visited by the Philippine Consul, who promised to help her. Eventually, she found a temporary home with a Filipino family who had settled in Britain.[63]

The number of those involved in these arrangements was uncertain. In 1998 there were said to be up to twenty thousand domestic workers in Britain who had entered the country in this way, most of them women from the Philippines, Bangladesh, India and Africa; at the beginning of the decade the figure was put at between two and three thousand. In 1996 a survey by Kalayaan, an organisation set up to campaign for justice for overseas domestic workers, reported that about half of them had to sleep on the floor, while four-fifths were either not paid regularly or received less than the agreed amount and some were locked in the house when the employer went out, to prevent them from running away. In a debate in the House of Lords in November 1990, Lord Hylton claimed that many saw only 'the airport, the employer's house and the road between the two'.[64] Several did escape, however, and unlike Sally, changed their identity and took other work illegally. Only those who stayed with their employer for four years had the opportunity to apply to remain in Britain indefinitely. Campaigners pressed for an alteration in the law to permit these vulnerable women to change employers during their first years of entry to the country, providing they agreed to remain in domestic employment and could produce evidence of ill-treatment. That was finally allowed in July 1998, but at the same time the rules were tightened. Henceforward, those whose duties were only cleaning, washing and cooking would not be eligible for admission with an employer. But any workers who did come in, for example to carry out childcare duties, would be free to change to another employer if they suffered abuse from their original master or mistress.[65] From the mid-1990s the minimum age of these workers was also raised from seventeen to eighteen.[66]

A number of women (and some men), who had entered the country in the normal way, also took cleaning jobs in public institutions and in offices and factories. Some did so because they had a poor command of English and so lacked the confidence, and perhaps the ability, to take up private domestic posts. However, for such workers, as for their British counterparts, the 1980s and early 1990s often witnessed a deterioration in employment conditions as a policy of privatising the cleaning of schools, hospitals and government buildings was pursued. The numbers involved were large, with an estimated 134,000 school cleaners and 36,000 cleaners employed in local government offices alone in 1982.[67] Where private contractors took over they often imposed more stringent working conditions than had applied under the previous direct labour arrangements. In Cambridgeshire, where over 1,200 school cleaners were made redundant in 1983 when the work was contracted out, workers' hours were cut from thirty-four to twenty per week and the time allocated to clean each classroom was halved. The poor standard of work and the rapid staff turnover that resulted led the county council to revert to direct labour when the two-year contract ended in 1985.[68] But many other local authorities persisted, because of the apparent cash savings offered by the process, even when levels of performance declined.

One woman who worked for many years as an office cleaner employed directly by the civil service compared the new contract arrangements unfavourably. As she declared bitterly: 'nobody checks to see what's going on.

And there's no doubt that cleaning standards go down with contract labour. You can't do the job properly when staff are always changing. There's got to be a lot of money being made by contractors, but it's not going to the cleaners.' Problems were particularly acute in places like airports, where twenty-four hour service had to be provided. In 1984 a report claimed that Asian workers at Heathrow Airport had to work rotating and irregular shifts without weekends off, sometimes having to cover a thirteen-and-a-half hour day at short notice, just to keep their jobs.[69] Eleven years later, a report by the European Commission declared that unlike virtually all the other countries in the European Union, the United Kingdom had no national collective working time or wage agreements for the cleaning sector. 'In effect, only a very small proportion of the estimated 200,000 contract-cleaning workforce is covered by any form of regulation related to these aspects of employment.'[70]

Not until the very end of the century did this situation begin to change, notably with the introduction of the National Minimum Wage in 1999. Research conducted by the Low Pay Commission concluded that this sector had been a particular beneficiary from that initiative, with companies encouraged 'to tender for contracts' on the basis of 'the service they can provide rather than how little they pay their staff'.[71] However, there were also those who sought to flout the spirit of the legislation. One cleaner who received the minimum wage was told by her employer that he expected her to work a great deal harder to earn it. He threatened to 'make something for you to do every minute of the day from now on'. The woman left because she found his attitude so aggressive.[72]

Finally, the increase in the number of rich people in the 1980s and 1990s also revived the demand for multi-staff households. Only in the economic recession of the early 1990s did this process slow down for a time. Lynn Brittney quotes households which had formerly hired a cook-housekeeper, a nanny, a chauffeur and a gardener now recruiting a separate cook as well as the housekeeper. In other cases, there was a demand for butlers or stewards who would also take over administrative responsibility for the running of the household. An advertisement in *The Lady* in January 2000 gives an indication of what was expected:

HOUSE STEWARD AND HOUSEKEEPER – Married couple required for a privately owned stately home in Cheshire. The House Steward will be responsible for the cleaning, care and preservation of this historic house and its contents. A major part of the job will concern the opening of the house both to the public and for corporate events. Further duties will include general maintenance and security. The Housekeeper will be jointly responsible for hall tours, including cooking and baking, and would also be required to carry out domestic cleaning for the owner on a regular basis. During term time may be expected to drive the owner's 8 year old son to school. In addition weekly babysitting will be required. This is a demanding position for a couple who have a flexible approach to their work and significant previous experience of working to the highest possible standard unsupervised. Own car and clean driving licences are essential. This is a live-in post with attractive spacious accommodation within the main building: The applicants will be non-smokers, physically fit and have no dependent children or dogs, although a love of dogs is a must. Salary to be negotiated. Must have impeccable references.[73]

Since few butlers or stewards were now being trained in households, other than those attached to the royal palaces, a number of 'schools' appeared designed to meet this need. Among the best known was Ivor Spencer's, which started in 1981 and at the end of the century was advertising its services on the internet.[74] In 2000 fees of £4,500 were charged for a six week course, which did not include food and accommodation. The aim was

to teach students to become first-class Butler Administrators/ Personal Assistants, with the object of taking control of a household or households, and . . . be responsible for the purchasing of food and wines including Champagne, cigars and clothes, booking travel for employers, and hiring of all staff. The School also teaches students how to organise large and small parties. . . . The salary Butlers usually receive when they commence a position is £25,000 Sterling per year in the UK. In the United States the starting salary per year is usually US $45,000, and elsewhere a similar wage structure, plus usually good accommodation, food, medical care, and a car for shopping.[75]

Students came from a varied background. In the late 1980s a survey of sixteen trainees then completing a course revealed that one was a former senior civil servant from Northern Ireland, another was a former member of the Household Cavalry and a third was an ex-cattle feed merchant from Leicester who had taken early retirement. He was the son of a butler and a cook and had been born on a landed estate in Sussex. With these antecedents he proved an apt learner and when the course ended he obtained a lucrative post in the United States.[76] In addition, in order to cater for *nouveaux riches* employers who had no experience of managing a domestic staff, Ivor Spencer ran short courses to guide them on how to handle servants. Without this, relations between the two parties could easily deteriorate, as staff resented what they regarded as their employer's unreasonable demands and the employer complained of uncooperative and sullen domestics.[77]

Early in 1998 the Lady Apsley School for Butlers was opened in a manor house near Cirencester, with five men in mid-to late middle age joining the first course. Each had paid £3,000 to be there and instruction was provided by a former under-butler at Buckingham Palace, who had spent the preceding two years as a gentleman's gentleman to a continental employer and had also run an English family's London home. The course lasted eight weeks, with the prospective butlers being schooled in everything from flower arranging to organising a cocktail party, polishing silver and ordering travel tickets and wine on the internet. At the end of the course there was to be an examination with a practical test at a real dinner party. The School was the brainchild of Sara Apsley, the daughter-in-law of the 8th Earl Bathurst and it was run in her home. 'Houses like this no longer have the full complement of staff', she declared, 'but sometimes we really do need properly trained staff, particularly butlers. After the sloppy eighties, people are starting to regain their sense of tradition and style.'[78] Interestingly, one estimate suggested in that year that there were only about 400 professional butlers in the whole country.[79]

Many men, though, took up these posts with little or no formal training. The philosophy of 'anyone will have to do' became the order of the day.[80] When Arthur Inch retired from the Kleinwort family's service in 1980, he and his wife were followed by a married couple who came as butler and cook and had previously run a public house. They remained for ten years before they, too, retired.

Often, however, the well-to-do opted for just one resident domestic, recruiting extra staff when necessary for special occasions. Ater Mr Inch retired, he began to go out on a free-lance basis to arrange luncheons, dinners and drinks parties in this way: 'My wife came out with me for many years . . . now my daughter often helps me', he wrote in 1999.[81] But he was saddened by the fact that once he and the few other remaining pre-war trained butlers had died out, there would be no one 'to take over and carry on the traditions of three to four hundred years of the science of domestic service which helped greatly the art of gracious living'.[82] These skills, he clearly felt, could not be learned in a few weeks at a special training school, but were the product of years of experience and of a steady progression up the domestic promotion ladder.

Even in the 1960s, when Peter Russell became butler to the Duke of Gloucester and later the Duke of Kent, he remembered the difficulty of keeping staff, particularly in the Gloucesters' country house. 'I took it to be the changing times. If things were bad in London, they were worse in the country. Who was going to cut themselves off from town life? It became difficult to replace staff.'[83] Peter himself entered private service after a spell as a batman/waiter in the 1950s when he was doing his National Service. He later became butler to the Chief Officer of the air base where he was stationed. Soon after leaving the Royal Air Force he went to an agency, Town and Country, near Sloane Square, to seek a post as a butler. He was told that the Duchess of Kent had a vacancy for an under-butler at Kensington Palace.[84] He took the post and thereby began his connection with the royal family. Yet, he, too, tired of the life in the 1960s and decided to accept a post with a large catering company in Essex. Not until the early 1980s did he revive his old skills by taking engagements as a contract butler.[85]

These, then, were the realities of servant life at the end of the twentieth century. In the large houses, staffs were much reducd and daily and contract workers had become an essential part of the domestic scene. The main growth area had become the households of the elderly and the affluent middle class, with their need for cleaners and for childcare providers. Admittedly, there were still large estates like Chatsworth, where longstanding, loyal servants were at work, but such examples were increasingly rare in a society governed by market forces and a growing sense of egalitarianism.

It is perhaps symbolic that Lynn Brittney, in her *Guide to Domestic Help* felt it necessary to warn employers of such potential dishonesties as the chauffeur who hired himself and his employers' car out for weddings when they were away and the housekeeper who purchased food and household articles out of her budget and then returned some of them to the shop in order to claim the refund for herself, or else she sold items to her friends.[86] Outside the pages of advice books there was also the case of the butler who faced a gaol sentence after selling his employer's Bentley car and hiring his own butler, while he pretended to be master of the house and entertained his friends from the public house.[87] However, even the Edwardians had complained of cooks who stole food from their mistresses and accepted bribes from tradesmen in return for placing orders with them.[88] Perhaps these later dishonesties were merely a sign that in the rapidly changing world of twentieth-century domestic service some old habits died hard.

HOTELS AND CATERING

The growing affluence of certain sectors of British society not only stimulated demand for domestic help but, coupled with an expansion in tourism, contributed greatly to the growth in the number and size of hotels and restaurants in the 1980s and 1990s. In the mid-1990s one estimate suggested that between 1979 and 1994 there had been almost a 27 per cent rise in the total of hotel and catering jobs in the country.[89] That trend was predicted to continue into the new century.[90] The new posts included kitchen staff, chambermaids, cleaners, waiters and bar staff and some at least involved people who in earlier decades would have become private servants. The speed of the expansion in the hospitality sector is indicated by the rise in the number of chefs and cooks during the 1980s. At a time when the total population of Great Britain grew by about 2.5 per cent, the number of male chefs and cooks increased by 44 per cent, with around three-fifths of them working in hotels and catering, according to the 10 per cent sample of economic activity published in the 1981 and 1991 population censuses.[91] Among female chefs and cooks the expansion was far smaller – at about 13.4 per cent – but significantly only a little over two-fifths of the women worked in the hospitality industry. The rest were employed in schools, factory canteens and public institutions. The total number of waiters and bar staff likewise grew by 56 per cent in the 1980s, while the increase in the number of waitresses was only about 5 per cent. However, as with household cleaning, the casual, part-time nature of much of the work probably seriously under-estimated the true female contribution.

A survey of hotels and catering in the mid-1980s estimated that around two-thirds of the labour force was female, with three-quarters of them working part-time. It also concluded that the women's contribution tended to be 'ghettoised', so that, for example, chambermaids were mostly female. In the kitchens, too, women normally carried out the least skilled jobs.[92] Indeed, some leading chefs insisted that the members of their team should all be male, as they considered that women were unable to withstand the heat and the pressure that went with producing high quality dishes for a discerning and demanding clientele.[93]

Immediately after the end of the Second World War, efforts were made to expand employment in hotels and catering in order to promote tourism and to attract overseas visitors with their much-needed foreign currency. 'The work is full of interest', declared one promotional leaflet encouragingly, 'especially to those who are fond of preparing food, cooking it or helping people in personal ways.'[94] However, it was only in the final quarter of the century that changing attitudes and growing demand brought about rapid modernisation and expansion in the sector as a whole.

The calibre of staff employed in any hotel or restaurant was a major factor in establishing its reputation. Indeed, an account of the Grosvenor House Hotel in London argued that in no other industry were staff-customer relations of greater importance. 'It is not, an exaggeration to say that the popularity of a hotel depends to a large extent on the quality of the personal service. In a luxury hotel this is especially important because one of the main qualifications of "luxury" is good room service.'[95]

That certainly applied to leading hotels like the Savoy in London, which prided itself upon its 'house-party atmosphere'. One of its directors claimed: 'We are the only hotel in London where every whim of the most exacting guests can be gratified at four in the morning as satisfactorily as at four in the afternoon.'[96] That meant employing a staff of over one thousand to attend to the needs of around five hundred guests. As Stanley Jackson declared in his highly flattering account of the Savoy, no hotel, 'however well-equipped and impressive, can function to perfection for twenty-four hours a day, year after year, without an enormous variety of gifted experts'.[97] When he wrote in the early 1960s, every floor was self-contained and was staffed by a housekeeper and a team of waiters, valets, chambermaids and cleaners.

In the 1980s and 1990s a growing number of hotels aimed to meet similarly exacting standards. They included Cliveden, which was opened in the Astors' former country house and sought to maintain much of the atmosphere of its illustrious past. One visitor to Cliveden in 1999 described it as offering 'the fantasy of country house luxury':

Today's rich may no longer have staff living in their houses, but they are still paying servants to look after them – the only difference is that now they buy their services piecemeal. . . . When a butler in coat tails appeared on the gravel to take our bags, there was no requirement to check in; he simply took our coats and led us across the great hall, up sweeping stairs, to our room. . . . By the time we were inside four or five members of staff had volunteered to open doors and so forth.[98]

When she and her partner went to dinner, 'young men glided around the table. There was nothing to be done, beyond picking up our own knife and fork.' In the meantime, 'maids were upstairs turning down the sheets, drawing the curtains, and placing slippers and mats by the bed. At four o'clock in the morning, I called down to the butler's pantry for a sandwich. Ten minutes later a young man appeared with it; the cucumber slices had been freshly peeled.' The next day, as they drove away, they saw two gardeners standing on the verge, leaning on their rakes. 'As we passed, they doffed their caps.' This was, of course, service on the grand scale, which few people could afford to experience at £500 a night for two.

At the same time there was a growth of non-British speciality restaurants with their own characteristic cuisines, be they European or from the Far East. Most were staffed by nationals of the appropriate countries, whose working conditions were, on the whole, negotiated within their own ethnic communities.

For many of those working in the over-heated atmosphere of a kitchen, however, the attraction soon faded. The rigours of being on duty in these conditions for up to sixteen hours a day on occasion, led to a catalogue of illnesses, including bad backs, sore feet, dermatitis, varicose veins and high blood pressure.[101] Tempers grew short and many 'celebrity chefs' adopted a bullying approach towards junior members of their brigades. One top London chef resigned at the end of the 1990s after he had branded a kitchen worker with a hot knife. Earlier he had stated that Michelin stars were 'the only reason' he worked as a chef; to get three was 'the only thing that I've wanted in my life'. He had, some time before, been the youngest chef in Britain to be awarded two Michelin stars, but the constant striving for excellence had created a destructive intolerance towards others.[102]

Part of this tension could be attributed to the devastating effect which the loss of a Michelin star or the appearance of an unenthusiastic entry in *The Good Food Guide*, could have on a chef and on the owner or, the manager of the restaurant. In 1996-7 the proprietor of a highly rated hotel in Taunton described in his diary the care with which a new edition of *The Good Food Guide* was perused: 'The write-up was pretty up-beat . . . except for a couple of lines which suggested that ours was "classic, safe cooking" that lacked the "adventure of British provincial cooking".' The real blow came early in January 1997 with the arrival of the new *Michelin Red Guide*. This revealed that the hotel had lost its 'precious star', which it had first gained in 1984. 'The news is so fresh', wrote the owner in his diary, '. . . that the shock of it has not sunk in. I feel strangely numb.'[103] The chef immediately offered to resign and although this was not accepted a thorough post-mortem was conducted to find out what had gone wrong.

These were problems faced by workers at the upper end of the market. For the majority of hotel staff, however, the difficulties they experienced were not related to the winning of prestigious awards, but those associated with long working hours, poor pay and insecurity of tenure, in an industry plagued by fluctuating demand and seasonal variations. Many workers in seaside or other holiday resort hotels were recruited for a few months in the year only, as had always been the case, and might be expected to take on a wide range of duties if they were working in a small business. Typical of many were the Ullswater hoteliers who were looking 'for an energetic, outgoing personality to join us for the summer season, to help in all departments'.[104] Then there was the proprietor of a Devon hotel who wanted 'Seasonal staff . . . for small family run hotel. Housekeeping, restaurant and assistant to chef. Good sense of humour and thick skin essential.'[105] It is not clear if the 'thick skin' was needed to cope with the management or the guests, but many members of hotel staffs had to learn to accept with equanimity the arrogance and unreasonable demands of some customers. One worker from the north-west of England commented bitterly that she considered that she and her fellow workers should be better paid because 'of the unsociable hours we have to work, the snobs we have to put up with and the painted smiles we always have to wear!!!'[106] Another also disliked the long and unsociable hours, but most resented the fact that the majority of the public 'look down upon us and treat us like general dogsbodies'.[107] Such comments were similar to those made by domestic workers in private service over half a century earlier.

At the end of the twentieth century even the *Caterer and Hotelkeeper*, a trade journal, referred to the industry's poor labour relations, with 'chefs, waiters and other hospitality staff . . . four times as likely to get the sack as workers in other jobs. They are also the most likely to quit.'[108] The high turnover of employees was pinpointed in the mid-1990s by a regional study of the north-west which suggested over a quarter of those surveyed had had three or more jobs within two years. Many had moved voluntarily, but others had had to leave because they were made redundant.[109] One hotel group attributed its own high staff turnover to 'the large growth in the Leisure and Hospitality sectors', with workers presumably looking around in order to better themselves. In this particular group each hotel averaged about 150 bedrooms and staff numbers were divided between around one hundred full timers and ninety casual or occasional workers.[110]

Also indicative of the difficult labour relations in the industry was its resistance to trade unionism, although unionism was in any case hampered by the rapid turnover of employees and the large number of casual workers. Nevertheless, in 1985 Lord Forte, then head of a multi-million-pound hotel and catering empire, expressed a common attitude when he claimed that by 'natural process' his business had reduced union membership from 36 per cent to 3 per cent.[111] Within the industry as a whole, at that date, union members comprised around 6 per cent of the total workforce, one of the lowest proportions in any industry.[112]

A combination of part-time and casual labour, a high level of staff turnover, employer hostility to unionism and the large number of relatively small workplaces left most of the staff in a 'strait-jacket of low pay, poor conditions and overall insecurity'.[113] The widespread use of young people to fill part-time posts reinforced this. Students were thought likely to encourage younger customers with money to spend and were also highly flexible. As one hotelier put it, he felt free 'to ring them and say it's not very busy', so they need not come in. 'I don't feel guilty about it . . . if they want a night off they say to me "Can I swap tomorrow night?"'[114]

Young workers were also relatively cheap, even after the introduction of the National Minimum Wage, since the pay for 18 to 21-year-olds was set at just £3 an hour and for those under 18 no minimum was set. Few of these young, casual employees intended to make a career in catering. They were merely looking to earn some cash while they were at school or college.

Most hotels, however, adopted a mixed age strategy for part-time workers. Older females, including members of ethnic minorities, were recruited to carry out the duties of chambermaids, cleaners and waitresses, particularly for breakfasts. Youngsters were thought to be less reliable at getting up in the morning than older staff.[115] The young people would then work 'unsocial' hours in the evenings and at weekends, or be expected to fill in as and when it was busy. A hotel general manager from the Manchester area described his own mixed-age policy in the late 1990s:

Food service is predominantly 16-19, bars 18-21, housekeeping and room attendants 25 plus and kitchen porters 40 plus.[116]

Training for casual or part-time workers was often rudimentary, not least because of the high staff turnover, and when it did take place it concentrated on basic food and hygiene issues, plus guidance on 'customer care' and sales techniques. The introduction of the National Minimum Wage boosted the pay of a number of adult females in the industry, although a few employers responded by charging for meals which had formerly been provided free, or by making an accommodation charge to those who lived in.[117] But for many non-resident part-timers there was a clear gain.

Despite this modest improvement, however, the pay and conditions of most workers in hotels and catering were still poor at the end of the century. Their position contrasted starkly with that of the small number of 'celebrity' chefs who not only commanded high salaries and great prestige, but might be able to secure lucrative television contracts and large royalties from the sale of books of recipes and reminiscences. On a broader front, the industry formed part of the important tourism sector and it provided growing employment opportunities for a number of people who might once have entered private service. That applied particularly to those in the kitchens and in the housekeeping department. One leading

London hotelier even claimed that hotel housekeeping was 'home housewifery on a large scale'.[118] providing a further example of the changing face of domestic employment in the second half of the twentieth century. Also significant in that context was the banishing of the words 'servant' and 'maid' from the domestic vocabulary and their replacement by 'helper' and 'assistant'.

Undoubtedly, a greater spirit of egalitarianism existed in 2000 than had applied a century earlier, but in terms of cash rewards and even social status there still remained much to reform if those supplying these important personal services were to receive adequate recognition. Despite the fond hopes of reformers from the 1920s onwards, domestic work has remained largely the preserve of the untrained and poorly paid. Violet Markham's strongly expressed desire in 1955 that it would be reorganised 'as a skilled craft with status, hours and wages comparable with those in other occupations' was still very largely unfulfilled at the end of the century.[119]

NOTES

Some abbreviations used

ARC = Archival Resource Centre at the University of Essex

GFS = Girls' Friendly Society

Hansard = Debates in the House of Commons, unless otherwise indicated

IWMSA = Imperial War Museum Sound Archives

LMA = London Metropolitan Archives

MHM = Market Harborough Museum

NVA = National Vigilance Association

MRC = Modern Records Centre at the University of Warwick

PP = Parliamentary Papers

PRO = Public Record Office i.e. National Archives

SHOHT = Shugborough Hall Oral History Transcripts: Staffordshire County Council

TUCL = Trades Union Congress Library at the London Metropolitan University

URA = University of Reading Archives
YWCA =Young Women's Christian Association

PART ONE

1   Marsh, *The Changing Social Structure*, p. 54.

2   *General Report of the 1951 Census of Population for England and Wales* (London, 1958), p.168. *Census of Population for England and Wales for 1951: Occupations* (London, 1956). *Census of Population for England and Wales for 1931: Occupations* (London, 1934).

3   *Census of Population for Scotland for 1951* (Edinburgh, 1956). The census estimated that the number of indoor domestic servants in Scotland had fallen by 46 per cent compared to 1931. (p. ix).

4   *Report on Post-War Organisation of Private Domestic Employment*, PP 1944--45, Vol. V, p.7. This report is hereafter referred to as the *Markham-Hancock Report*.

5   Mrs L. Buckley of Kettering to Violet Markham, 29 March 1946 in Markham MSS. 12/3.

6   Powell, *Below Stairs*, p. 154.

7   See *Ministry of Labour Gazette*, October 1951.

8   Summerfield, *Women Workers in the Second World*

War, p. 31.

9　Robinson, *Country House at War*, pp. 12-13,46-8.

10　H. Jones (ed.), *Duty and Citizenship*, p. 150.

11　Waugh, *Put Out More Flags*, pp. 11-12,74. First published in 1942.

12　*The Lady*, 27 March 1941.

13　Robinson, *Country House at War*, p. 28.

14　T. Humphris, *Garden Glory*, pp. 101, 154, 157-8, 160, 161.

15　*The Times*, 6 August 1941. *The Lady*, 3 April 1941. *Country Life*, 8 February 1941.

16　*Census of Population for England and Wales for 1951: Occupations* and *Census of Population for Scotland for 1951*.

17　*Country Life*, 4 January 1941. T. W. Turner, *Memoirs of a Gamekeeper*, pp. 75, 78. Mursell, *Come Dawn, Come Dusk*, pp. 111, 113-14.

18　Mursell, *Come Dawn, Come Dusk*, p. 118.

19　*Censuses of Population for England and Wales and for Scotland, 1931* and 1951.

20　Nudds, *Woods Belong to Me*, p. 60.

21　Inch, *Reminiscences*, pp. 115-16.

22　P. Horn, *Rise and Fall of the Victorian Servant*, p. 201.

23　R. Harrison, *Rose*, pp. 179, 186,203.

24　IWMSA, 11813.

25　Ibid.

26   Partridge, *Pacfist's War*, pp. 84, 91.

27   Summerfield, *Reconstructing Women's Wartime Lives*, p. 89, 307.

28   Pugh, *Women and the Women's Movement*, p. 274.

29   Balderson with Goodlad, *Backstairs Life*, p. 89.

30   Summerfield, *Reconstructing Women's Wartime Lives*, pp. 146,306.

31   Summerfield, *Women Workers in the Second World War*, pp. 34, 61.

32   Ibid, pp. 34-6. Briar, *Working for Women?* p. 75.

33   Thoms, *War, Industry and Society*, p. 47.

34   *Hansard*, 5th Series, Vol. 377, 27 January 1942, col. 566 and *Hansard*, 5th Series, Vol. 381, 21 July 1942, cols 1402-1403. Summerfield, *Women Workers in the Second World War,* p.49.

35   *Hansard*, 5th Series, Vol. 377, 27 January 1942, col. 377.

36   *The Times*, 15 February 1943.

37   Partridge, *Pacifist's War*, pp. 179, 181.

38   Quoted in Summerfield, *Women Workers in the Second World War*, p. 49.

39   *The Lady*, 20 February 1941.

40   *Hansard*, 5th Series, Vol. 383, 22 October 1942, cols 2072-2073.

41   Draft letter from Violet Markham to Ernest Bevin, n.d. [1943] in Markham MSS. 12/2.

42   *Hansard*, 5th Series, Vol. 377, 27 January 1942, col.

566.

43 *Report of the Royal Commission on Population*, Cmd. 7695 (London, 1949), pp. 182-3.

44 *The Times*, 20 February 1943.

45 *Hansard*, 5th Series, Vol. 403, 18 October 1944, col. 2402.

46 *Report of the Royal Commission on Population*, 185. See also Violet Markham draft letter to Ernest Bevin [1943] In Markham MSS., 12/2, section on home helps.

47 Hunt and Fox, *The Home Help Service in England and Wales*, SS.407 (London, 1970), p. 3. E. S. Turner, *What the Butler Saw*, p. 294.

48 Mrs Mary Cocking of West Hoathly, Sussex, in correspondence with the author, 24 April and 5 May 1999.

49 Ibid., 24 April and 12 May 1999.

50 Letter from Mrs Sheila Chugg of Braunton Devon, to the author, 1 July 1999.

51 Ibid., n.d. [*c*. July 1999].

52 Violet Markham to Ernest Bevin, 19 April 1943, on 'Proposals for a Domestic Service Corps' in LAB.25/188, PRO.

53 Ibid.

54 Minutes from Miss Mary Smieton, 8 July 1943 and from Mrs A. C. M. Gulland, 7 July 1943 in LAB.25/189 at the PRO.

55 *Hansard*, 5th Series, Vol. 403, 18 October 1944,

col. 2402. Elliott, *The Status of Domestic Work in the United Kingdom with Special Reference to the National Institute of Houseworkers* (Geneva, 1951), p. 7. Violet Markham to Mary Smieton, 18 October 1943, in Markham MSS. 12/2.

56 Dorothy M. Elliott, ibid., p. 7.

57 'Memorandum on Post-War Britain of the Domestic Worker', produced by a Sub-Committee of Domestic Workers and TUC Women's Advisory Committee in Minutes of the National Union of Domestic Workers at MRC, MSS.292/54.76/57.

58 *Markham-Hancock Report*, pp. 3, 7-8,19.

59 See letter from Violet Markham to *The Times*, 15 January 1955.

60 *Markham-Hancock Report*, pp. 11-16,21. .

61 *Report of the Interdepartmental Committee on the Care of Children*, PP 1945-46, Vol. X, pp. 71,174. Briar, *Working for Women?* p. 85.

62 *Eighty-first Annual Report of Dr Barnardo's Homes for 1946*, (London, 1947), p. 13.

63 Information provided by Dr Barnardo's Homes. The Annual Reports of Dr Barnardo's Homes also confirm the decline in domestic servant or housecraft training in the post-war years.

64 J. Rose, *For the Sake of the Children*, pp. 200-1.

65 *The Times*, 2 February 1946. See also Violet Markham, typescript on 'Domestic Work', 22 January 1946, in which she referred to the 'alarming'

effect on the birth-rate 'of the difficulties of making and keeping a home'. In Markham MSS., 12/9.

66 Lewis & Maude, *The English Middle Classes*, p. 256. First published in 1949.

67 See the *Population Census Reports for England and Wales*, for 1931, 1951 and 1961.

68 Powell, *Below Stairs*, p. 156.

69 [Anon. ed.], *Mrs Beeton's Household Management*, p. viii.

70 P. Horn, *Rise and Fall of the Victorian Servant*, p. 202.

71 Waterson (ed.), *Country House Remembered*, pp. 193-4.

72 Stokes, *Norland*, pp. 105, 109-10.

73 *Newsletter of the National Union of Domestic Workers*, October 1950, at MRC, MSS.292/54.76/28.

74 Letter from Arthur R. Inch to the author, 15 December 1999.

75 Mullins & Griffiths, *Cap and Apron*, pp. 37-8.

76 In five issues of *The Lady* in January 1948 there were 159 domestic advertisements in all, including some for hotels and catering establishments. In the *The Lady* for 8 January 1959, there were 265 vacancies for private domestic staff advertised. There was a separate section for hotels and commercial premises. On 26 February 1959, 226 vacancies were advertised. Vacancies for mother's helps were

mentioned, but the main emphasis was on cooks, nannies and occasionally, married couples.

77 Ellis (ed.), *Thatched with Gold*, p. 240. Violet Markham, TS on 'Domestic Work', (Markham MSS., 12/9), referred to women taking 'refuge in hotels and boarding-houses'.

78 Waterson (ed.), *Country House Remembered*, pp. 246-8.

79 Duchess of Devonshire, *House*, pp. 69, 74-6, 78.

80 Ibid., pp. 78-82.

81 Ibid., p. 78.

82 John, Duke of Bedford, *Silver-plated Spoon*, pp. 17-18, 180,203.

83 T. Humphris, *Garden Glory*, pp. 163, 164, 174.

84 Gregory, *Gardener's Life*, pp. 54-6, 58, 60, 62-3, 72.

85 Eley, *Here is Mr Streeter*, p. 127.

86 E. S. Turner, *What the Butler Saw*, p. 293. *The Times*, 8 February 1946.

87 Elliott, *Status of Domestic Work*, p. 9. The NIH was established under the Companies Act of 1929 as a company limited by guarantee and not having share capital. See 'The National Institute of Houseworkers', extract from the *Ministry of Labour Gazette* for October 1951, in LAB.70/2 at the PRO.

88 *Training Scheme for Houseworkers: National Institute of Houseworkers* (London, n.d. [c. 1947])

at the TUCL, HD.6072.

89   Elliott, *Status of Domestic Work*, p. 21.

90   *The National Institute of Houseworkers Limited: Press Information* (1963) in LAB.70/2 at the PRO.

91   Elliott, *The Status of Domestic Work*, 17-19 and *Annual Reports of the Ministry of Labour and National Service* for 1948, PP 1948-49, Vol. XVII, pp. 46-7 and for 1949, PP 1950, Vol. XII, p. 38.

92   *The Employer and the Worker in Private Domestic Work*, issued by the NIH, n.d., at MRC, MSS.292/54.76/61. Elliott, ibid., pp. 12-14.

93   *Hansard*, 5th Series, Vol. 487, 27 April 1951, col. 803.

94   *Houseworker*, September 1948 at MRC, MSS.292/54.76/62a. See also *Houseworker*, January 1948, commenting that the Oxford centre was the smallest of those established.

95   'Institute Training: Experience of Five Years' Working, September 1947-August 1952' at MRC, MSS.292/54.76/ 62b.

96   *Houseworker*, January 1948.

97   *Plan for the Girl who Loves Housework*, leaflet issued by the NIH (n.d.) in Markham MSS., 12/10.

98   *Annual Report of the Ministry of Labour and National Service for 1949*, p. 38.

99   Elliott, *The Status of Domestic Work*, p. 16.

100   Ibid., p. 10.

101   NIH: 'Report on the Pre-Diploma Year', 12 June
      1953, at MRC, MSS.292/54.76/62b.

102   Letter from Mrs S. Whiting (nee Chapman) to the
      author, 4 July 1999.

103   Letters from Mrs S. Whiting to the author, 4 and
      11 July 1999.

104   Elliott, *Status of Domestic Work*, p. 17.

105   *The Times*, 7 November 1952, Marsh, *Changing
      Social Structure*, p. 147. *Annual Report of the
      Ministry of Labour for 1960*, PP 1960-61, Vol.
      XVIII, p. 34.

106   *Annual Report of the Ministry of Labour and
      National Service for 1949*, p. 38. NIH Ltd. 'Report on
      the London County Council Home Help Service', n.d.
      [*c*. 1949], in Markham MSS., 12/10.

107   Letter from Mrs S. Whiting to the author, 11 July
      1999.

108   Mrs Kathleen M. Cripps, JP to Miss Nancy Adam,
      Chief Woman Officer of the TUC, 9 January 1949
      at MRC, MSS.292/54.76/61.

109   *Hansard*, 5th Series, Vol. 487, 27 April 1951, cols.
      803-806. *Sunday Pictorial*, 16 January 1949,
      under the heading 'Servant Scheme Waste of
      Money'. 'Report on the Cost of Training Students'
      by Dorothy Elliott, 22 March 1949, at MRC,
      MSS.292/54.76/62a.

110   *Hansard*, 5th Series, Vol 509, 18 December 1952;

written answer, col. 227.

111   *Manchester Guardian*, 26 September 1951, report headed 'Room for Economy'.

112   *NIH Annual Report*, June 1949 in Markham MSS., 12/10.

113   *The Times*, 10 July 1952.

114   *Annual Reports of the Ministry of Labour and National Service for 1952*, PP 1952-53, Vol. XlV, p. 39 and for 1953, PP 1953-54, Vol. XVI, p. 39.

115   *Annual Report of the Ministry of Labour and National Service for 1950*, PP 1950-51, Vol. XVI, p. 41. *Annual Report of the National Institute for Housecraft (Employment and Training) Limited for 1965-66*, pp. 12-13 in LAB.70/62, PRO.

116   *NIH: Progress Report to 16 January, 1954* at MRC, MSS.292/54.76/62b. *Annual Report of the Ministry of Labour for 1960*, p. 34.

117   Hunt & Fox, *Home Help Service*, pp. 3, 9-10. *Annual Report of the NIH (Employment and Training) Limited for 1964-65*, p. 13, at the TUCL, HD.6072. *Annual Report of the National Institute for Housecraft (Employment and Training) Limited for 1965-66*, pp. 12-13.

118   *Houseworker*, May-June, 1954.

119   Ibid.

120   *Houseworker*, September 1949.

121   *Annual Report of the NIH for 1964-65*, p. 14.

122   Miss M. Brodie, Executive Director, NIH to

J. A. Doyle, Department of Employment and Productivity, Central Youth Employment Executive, 15 September 1970, PRO, LAB.70/9.

123 Miss M. Brodie to F. Pickford, Department of Employment, 16June 1972, PRO, LAB.70/11.

124 *Annual Report of the NIH for 1956-57*, 3-4, TUCL, HD.6072.

125 NIH, Memorandum to the Association of Education Committees, 20 August 1971, in LAB.70/11, PRO.

126 *Annual Report of the Ministry of Labour for 1959*, PP 1959-60, Vol. XVII, p. 49.

127 NIH (Employment and Training) Ltd. Points for discussion at an informal meeting on 13 January 1971, in LAB.70/10, PRO.

128 *Annual Report of the NIH for 1966-67*, pp. 7-12 listed some of the courses provided, TUCL, HD.6072.

129 *Annual Reports of the NIH for 1966-67*, p. 10 and 1964-65, p. 6.

130 The NIH (Employment and Training) Ltd. Points for discussion at an informal meeting on 13 January 1971, in LAB.70/10, PRO.

131 *Hansard*, 9 December 1971 in LAB.70/10, PRO. Letter from Robert Carr, Secretary of State for Employment to Baroness White, 17 January 1972, in LAB.70/11, PRO.

132 Miss M. Brodie, Executive Director, NIH to 3li

William Alexander, Association of Education Committees, 29 August 1972. *Final Report to Directors of the NIH (Employment and Training) Ltd, 19 September 1972*, both in LAB.70/11, PRO.

133 *Hansard*, 9 December 1971, in LAB.70/10, PRO.

134 Meetings held on 19 and 21 June 1945. See Minutes in LAB.8/1208, PRO.

135 Minute by Mrs Gulland of the Ministry of Labour and National Service, 4 June 1946 in LAB.8/1208, PRO.

136 Minute from Mrs Gulland, 6 July 1946 in LAB.26/163, PRO.

137 Consultative Committee on Recruitment of Domestic Workers for Hospitals: Minutes of meeting held on 29 May 1946 in LAB.26/163, PRO.

138 *Annual Report of the Ministry of Labour and National Service for 1947*, PP 1948-49, Vol. XVII, p. 42.

139 Consultative Committee on Recruittnent of Domestic Workers for Hospitals: Minutes of meeting held on 29 May 1946 in LAB.26/163, PRO.

140 *Annual Report of the Ministry of Labour and National Service for 1947*, pp. 42-3.

141 *Annual Reports of the Ministry of Labour and National Service for 1949*, pp. 20-1 and for 1950, pp. 21-2.

142 *Hansard*, 5th Series, Vol. 413, 24 August 1945, col.

413.

143 Sir Alexander Maxwell to Sir Godfrey Ince, 19 November 1945 in LAB.8/92, PRO. See also Minute by Sir Godfrey Ince, 11 September 1945, concerning a meeting with Lord Rushcliffe and the latter's desire to bring over a domestic worker from Holland, in LAB.8/1171.

144 Violet Markham to Mary Smieton at the Ministry of Labour and National Service, 8 March 1946, in LAB.8/1171.

145 *Hansard*, 5th Series, Vol. 421, 11 April 1946, col. 2112. Letter from CM. Lead, Overseas Department of the Ministry of Labour and National Service, to Miss Nancy Adam of the National Union of Domestic Workers, 19 March 1949, MRC, MSS.292/54.76/37.

146 *Annual Report of the Ministry of Labour and National Service for 1949*, p. 22. *Annual Report of the Ministry of Labour and National Service for 1939-46*, PP 1946-47, Vol. XII, p. 209.

147 *Hansard*, 5th Series, Vol. 462, 8 March 1949, cols. 964-965.

148 *Hansard*, 5th Series, Vol. 414, 18 October 1945, col. 1365 and *Hansard*, 5th Series, Vol. 421, 11 April 1946, col. 2112.

149 *Annual Report of the Ministry of Labour and National Service for 1948*, PP 1948-49, Vol. XVII, 26. Letter from C. M. Lead of the Overseas

Department of the Ministry of Labour and National Service to Miss Nancy Adam, of the NUDW, 31 December 1948, MRC, MSS.292/54.76/37.

150 C. M. Lead to Miss Nancy Adam, 31 December 1948, MRC, MSS.292/54.76/37.

151 Leaflet from Isobel Jay Ltd., International Employment Office, Hove, sent 9 June 1949 to Sir Walter Citrine at the Trades Union Congress, MRC, MSS.292/54.76/37.

152 See undated press cutting, MRC, MSS.292/54.76/37, noting that 'three million' German girls had 'no mathematical chance of getting a man at all' in their home country.

153 See undated press cutting (*c.* 1950) in MSS.292/54.76/37, MRC, MSS.292/54.76/37.

154 See cutting from the *Daily Mail* n.d. (*c.* 1952-53) in LAB.8/1905, PRO.

155 Waterson, *Servants' Hall*, pp. 200-1.

156 E.J. Toogood, Ministry of Labour and National Service to G.W.J. Cole, Councillor (Labour) British Embassy, 3 October 1956 in LAB.8/1905, PRO.

157 *Annual Report of the Ministry of Labour and National Service for 1950*, pp. 21, 28. 'Notes on the Scheme to provide a German Woman for resident domestic work in Great Britain' at MRC, MSS.292/54.76/37. 'Report on Private Domestic Workers Schemes, Germany and Austria', n.d. (*c.* 1954) in LAB.8/1905, PRO.

158 Minute on German P.D.W Scheme by Miss B.P. Boyes, 17 January 1952 and 'Report on Private Domestic Workers Schemes, Germany and Austria', both in LAB.8/1905, PRO.

159 Statement on the working of the German and Austrian schemes, 1954, in LAB.8/1905, PRO.

160 Dawes, 'The Dying Reign of the Pantry' in The *Daily Telegraph Magazine*, 6 July 1973, pp. 14-20.

161 Ibid., p. 16.

162 Dr Joyce Chalmers of Llangollen in correspondence with the author, 3 February 1999.

163 Mrs Helen Bell of Thatcham in correspondence with the author, 24 February 1999.

164 E.S. Turner, *What the Butler Saw*, pp. 295-6.

165 *Hansard*, 5th Series, Vol. 691, 16 March 1964, cols 976-977. One German *au pair* had five different places between April 1969 and January 1970; when her hosts asked her to leave, the first four invariably gave her just a few days' notice. Information and correspondence provided by Anne Jüssen, Frauen Museum, Bonn.

166 *Hansard*, 5th Series, Vol. 691, 16 March 1964, col. 976.

167 Briar, *Working for Women?* p. 111.

168 *Guardian*, 23 January 1993.

169 *Hansard*, 5th Series, Vol. 686, 16 December 1963, written answers, col. 150.

170 Patterson, *Dark Strangers*, pp 81, 135 6.

171 Minute by Miss Hanson, Ministry of Labour and National Service, 14 October 1952, refers to taking 'the coloured women in small parties' in LAB.8/6, PRO.

PART TWO

1 'At your service' in *The Economist*, 14 December 1996.

2 Brittney, *Which? Guide to Domestic Help*, p. 10.

3 Young, 'It's not hard to find good help these days' in *The Times*, 25 September 1998.

4 Brittney; *Which? Guide to Domestic Help*, pp. 19-20.

5 *Guardian*, 6 February 1990.

6 Ibid.

7 Chris Arnot, 'Stark Vision' in *Guardian: Society*, 26 July 2000.

8 Alfred Sherman, 'In-house training and the domestic service dilemma' in *Guardian*, 9 January 1984. Rosie Cox, The Role of Ethnicity, p. 134.

9 Gregson & Lowe, *Servicing the Middle Classes*, pp. 140-1.

10 'Younger Mrs Mopps sweep back into rooms at the top' in *The Times*, 6 January 1997.

11 Brittney, *Which? Guide to Domestic Help*, p. 142.

12 Cox, 'Exploring the Growth of Paid Domestic Labour: a case study of London', forthcoming in

Geography, p. 2. I am indebted to Rosie Cox of Coventry University for allowing me to see a copy of this paper ahead of publication.

13 Cox, 'The Role of Ethnicity', p. 138.

14 Pullinger & Summerfield (ed.), *Social Focus on Women and Men*, p. 28.

15 Gregson & Lowe, *Servicing the Middle Classes*, p. 50.

16 Ibid., pp. 96, 98-101.

17 Ibid., pp. 100-1.

18 *Guardian*, 6 February 1990. See also Nigella Lawson, 'Do you pay your Cleaner in Guilt' in *The Times*, 5 March 1997.

19 Brittney, *Which? Guide to Domestic Help*, p. 10.

20 Ibid., p. 23.

21 Matheson & Summerfield (ed.), *Social Focus on Older People*, p. 74. Brittney, *Which? Guide to Domestic Help*, pp. 30-3. *Oxford Times*, 11 February 2000.

22 'Paid to do the Dirty Work' in *Guardian*, 18 August 1992.

23 Mrs Sheila Whiting in correspondence with the author, 4 July 1999.

24 [Anon. ed.], *A People's Autobiography of Hackney*, p. 114.

25 Ibid., pp. 118-19.

26 Cox, 'Exploring the Growth of Paid Domestic Labour', p. 6.

27 'Nanny of the Year Award: 2000' in *The Lady*, 20-26 June 2000. Gregson & Lowe, *Servicing the Middle Classes*, p. 3.

28 William Weber in correspondence with the author, 18 July 1997.

29 Rachel Campbell Johnston, 'Life behind the green baize doors' in *The Times*, 11 July 1998. William Weber to the author, 25 August 2000.

30 Robin Young in *The Times*, 25 September 1998.

31 The Childcare Link was advertised in buses and other public places in 2000. *Need a Nanny? A guide for parents* (London: Department for Education and Employment, 1999). A list of member nanny and *au pair* agencies provided by the Federation of Employment and Recruitment Agencies was publicised on the Internet: www.fres.co.uk.

32 Details of Ivor Spencer's School were published on the Internet: www.ivorspencer.com/butler.htm.

33 Cox, 'The Role of Ethnicity', p. 137.

34 Gregson & Lowe, *Servicing the Middle Classes*, p. 196.

35 Ibid., p. 291.

36 *The Times*, 3 October 1998.

37 Mary Gold, 'Mrs Danvers' day has come' in *The Times*, 6 November 1999.

38 See *myhome* brochure (London, 2000) and Esther Addley, 'Are you being served', in *Guardian,* 16 March 2000.

39 Mary Gold in *The Times*, 6 November 1999.

40 Jane Shilling, 'In praise of housekeeping' in *The Times*, 27 September 1999.

41 Mary Gold in *The Times*, 6 November 1999.

42 *Guardian*, 7 March 2000.

43 Ibid.

44 Jane Ellison, 'Paying the price for nanny power' in *Sunday Correspondent*, 25 March 1990.

45 *The Times*, 19 January 1999.

46 Maureen Freely, 'We must do better than this' in *Guardian*, 20 January 1999. Gregson & Lowe, *Servicing the Middle Classes*, p. 5, note similar sensationalism in reaction to earlier cases involving nannies and their real or alleged mistreatment of their charges.

47 'Ministers to set up register for Nanny Agencies' in *The Times*, 17 January 2000.

48 *Need a Nanny?* p. 1.

49 *Hansard*, 6th Series, Vol. 327, 8 March 1999, col. 27.

50 Brittney, *Which? Guide to Domestic Help*, pp. 148-9 and information provided by the Home Office concerning *au pairs*, July 2000. *Hansard*, 6th Series, Vol. 326, 25 February 1999, cols. 629 and 634.

51 *Hansard*, 6th Series, Vol. 327, 8 March 1999, col. 27.

52 Cox, 'The Role of Ethnicity', pp. 135, 136, 140. *Hansard*, (House of Lords), 5th Series, Vol. 597, No.

32, 8 February 1999, col. 8. *The Times*, 21 January and 17 February 1999.

53 *Hansard* (House of Lords), 5th Series, Vol. 597, No. 32, 8 February 1999, cols. 8-10. See also *Hansard* (House of Lords), 5th Series, Vol. 565, 3 July 1995, col. 934, concerning illegal immigration from Poland.

54 *Guardian*, 23 January 1993.

55 Information and correspondence kindly provided by Anne Jüssen of the Frauen Museum, Bonn, to the author, 14 December 1999. Anne is Adele's friend.

56 Lipman, *How Was It For You?*, p. 5-6.

57 Plimmer, 'She's mad, not bad, but I despair' in *The Times*, 12 June 1999.

58 Frean, 'Minimum pay threatens end of the *au pair*' in *The Times*, 21 January 1999. See also correspondence in *The Times*, 27 and 30 January 1999.

59 Frean, '*Au pair* minimum wage rules dropped' in *The Times*, 17 February 1999. *Hansard*, 6th Series, Vol. 326, 25 February 1999, cols. 633-634.

60 Brittney, *Which? Guide to Domestic Help*, pp. 149-50.

61 Cox, 'The Role of Ethnicity', pp. 139-40. Phizacklea (ed.), *One Way Ticket*, p. 98.

62 Anderson, *Britain's Secret Slaves*, pp. 43, 44.

63 *Observer Magazine*, 28 January 1990, pp. 19-20. *Hansard*, (House of Lords), 5th Series, Vol. 523, 28

November 1990, cols. 1039 and 1046.

64   *Hansard,* (House of Lords), 5th Series, Vol. 523, 28
     November 1990, col. 1038. 'Foreigners Face Ban on
     Bringing in their Servants' in *The Times,* 21 August
     1997. 'Foreign servants get right to quit "slavery"'
     in *The Times,*10 February 1998.

65   *Hansard* (House of Lords), 5th Series, Vol. 592, 31
     July 1998, written answer, cols. 131-132. 'Foreign
     servants get right to quit "slavery"' in *The Times,*
     10 February 1998.

66   *Hansard* (House of Lords), 5th Series, Vol. 559,12
     December 1994, written answer, col. 108.

67   [Anon.] *The Contract Clean-up,* p. 10, in TUCL,
     HD.6072.

68   [Anon.] *Taken to the Cleaners,* p. 33 in TUCL,
     HD.6072.

69   *Community Action,* No. 67 (November 1984), pp.
     15-19 in TUCL, HD.6072.

70   *Statutory and Agreement-Based Provisions on
     Certain Aspects of the Organisation of Working
     Time in the Cleaning Industry. European Social
     Dialogue: Document Series* (Brussels, 1993), p. 17
     in TUCL, HD.6072.

71   *Second Report of the Low Pay Commission.
     The National Minimum Wage: The Story So Far,*
     Cm.4571 (London, 2000), pp. 48-9. From October
     2000 the minimum adult rate became £3.70 per
     hour.

72 *Guardian*, 26 July 2000.

73 *The Lady*, 11-17 January 2000. Brittney, *Which? Guide to Domestic Help*, p. 18.

74 Ivor Spencer's Internet site was www.ivorspencer. com/butler.htm.

75 See entry in Ivor Spencer's Internet site, June 2000.

76 *Guardian*, 28 December 1988.

77 'Butlers suffer as New Rich make poor Employers' in *The Times*, 26 July 1997.

78 *The Times*, 31 January 1998.

79 Robin Young in *The Times*, 25 September 1998.

80 R. Harrison (ed.), *Gentlemen's Gentlemen*, p. 243.

81 Arthur R. Inch in correspondence with the author, 15 December 1999.

82 Inch, *Reminiscences*, p. 116.

83 Russell, *Butler Royal*, pp. 181-2.

84 Ibid., pp. 24, 30-1.

85 Ibid., p. 204.

86 Brittney, *Which? Guide to Domestic Help*, p. 180.

87 'Butlers suffer as New Rich make poor Employers' in *The Times*, 26 July 1997.

88 P. Horn, *Rise and Fall of the Victorian Servant*, pp. 158-62.

89 Khan & Kirkham, *Behind the Painted Smiles*, p. 1.

90 *Second Report of the Low Pay Commission. The National Minimum Wage*, p. 45.

91   Calculated from the *1981 Census of Population of Great Britain: Economic Activity* (London, 1984), and *1991 Census of Population of Great Britain: Economic Activity*, Vol. 1 (London, 1994).

92   Byrne (ed.), *Waiting for Change?* Low Pay Pamphlet No. 42 (London, July 1986), pp. 9, 16.

93   Dominic Bradbury, 'Sexism over the stove' in *The Times*, 6 March 1999.

94   *'Personal Service' Careers for Boys and Girls in the Catering Industry* (London: Ministry of Labour and National Service, September 1946), p. 4, in the TUCL, HD.9999CH.6.

95   Jones & Hewitt, *A.H. Jones of Grosvenor House*, p. 112.

96   S. Jackson, *Savoy*, pp. 261, 287.

97   Ibid., p. 144. Contarini, *The Savoy was my Oyster*, pp. 49, 55.

98   Decca Aitkenhead, 'At 4 a.m. I wanted a sandwich' in *Guardian*, 5 January 1999.

99   Advertisement in *Caterer and Hotelkeeper*, 11-17 November 1999.

100   Joe Warwick, 'Waiting for a proper job' in *The Times*, 16 January 1999.

101   'Labour Pains' in *Caterer and Hotelkeeper*, 19-25 August 1999.

102   *The Times*, 16 December 1999. See also the third leader in *The Times* for this date. Sabine Durrant on Gordon Ramsay, 'chef of the year' in *Guardian*,

10 July 2000, for another example of the volatile temperament and bullying attitude of one of the top chefs.

103 'King of the Castle but in fear of those Michelin men' in *The Times*, 9 January 1999.

104 *The Lady*, 20-26 June 2000.

105 *The Lady*, 23 February to 1 March 1999.

106 Khan & Kirkham, *Behind the Painted Smiles*, p. 27.

107 Ibid., p. 27.

108 *Caterer and Hotelkeeper*, 23 December 1999 to 12 January 2000.

109 Khan & Kirkham, *Behind the Painted Smiles*, pp. 23, 25.

110 Nichola Roskell, Group Personnel Manager of Paramount Hotel Group in correspondence with the author, 27 June 2000.

111 Byrne (ed.), *Waiting for Change?* p. 47.

112 Ibid, p. 47.

113 Ibid., p. 53.

114 *The Low Paid and the Minimum Wage* by the Low Pay Unit, Vol. 3 (London: Low Pay Unit, n.d. [*c.* 1999]), p. 20.

115 Ibid., pp. 17, 20.

116 Ibid., p. 17.

117 *Second Report of the Low Pay Commission, The National Minimum Wage*, pp. 45 and 47. *The Low Paid and the Minimum Wage*, p. 37.

118 Goring, *50 Years of Service*, p. 99.

119 *The Times*, 13 January 1955; letter from Miss Markham. See also Gregson & Lowe, *Servicing the Middle Classes*, pp.233-5.

BIBLIOGRAPHY

N.B. Only printed sources are given here. All manuscript and oral history material used has been detailed in the footnotes.

OFFICIAL PAPERS

Report of the Interdepartmental Committee on Care of Children (1945-46)

Home Office, *Report on the work of the Children's Branch, April 1923* (1923) and *Fifth Report on the work of the Childrens Branch, January 1938* (1938)

Hunt, A. and Fox, J. *The Home Help Service in England and Wales* (1970)

Ministry of Labour, *Annual Reports* (1924-25 to 1960-61)

Ministry of Labour, *Report to the Minister of Labour of the Committee on the Supply of Female Domestic Servants* (1923)

Ministry of Labour, *Second Interim Report of the Central*

Committee on Women's Training and Employment for the Period ending 31 December 1922 (1923)

Local Government Board, *Annual Report for 1911* (1912-13)

Second Report of Low Pay Commission, *The National Minimum Wage: The Story So Far* (2000)

Need a Nanny? A Guide for Parents (1999)

Report of Oversea Settlement Committee, for year ending 31 December 1922 (1923)

Reports of Population Censuses for England and Wales and Scotland (1901-1991)

Royal Commission on Population (1949)

Report on Post-War Organisation of Private Domestic Employment, Violet Markham and Florence Hancock (1944-45)

Reports to President of the Oversea Settlement Committee on Openings for Women in Canada (1919); in Australia (1920); and in New Zealand (1920)

Ministry of Reconstruction, *Report of the Women's Advisory Committee on the Domestic Service Problem* (1919)

Annual Reports of the Chief Inspector of Reformatory and Industrial Schools of Great Britain, for 1912 and 1915

Report of the Departmental Committee Appointed to Enquire on Land in Scotland, Used as Deer Forests (1922)

Royal Commission on Unemployment Insurance; Majority and Minority Reports (1931-32)

NEWSPAPERS AND JOURNALS

Blackpool Gazette, Houseworker, British Boarding-House Proprietor, Labour Woman, Caterer and Hotelkeeper, The Lady, Country Life, Lancet, Daily Mail, London Evening Standard, Daily News, Manchester Guardian, Domestic Servants' Advertiser, Ministry of Labour Gazette, Economist, Observer, The Field, The Times, Gardeners' Chronicle, YWCA Newsletter, GFS Magazine, Good Housekeeping, Hansard, Guardian.

BOOKS AND ARTICLES

A Few Rules for the Manners of Servants in Good Families (London, 1895)

Anderson, B. *Britain's Secret Slaves. An Investigation into the Plight of Overseas Domestic Workers* (Anti-Slavery International Human Rights Series, No.5, 1993)

Anderson, W. *A Rather Special Place. Growing up in Cardiff Dockland* (Llandysul, 1993)

Astor, M. *Tribal Feeling* (London, 1963)

Balderson, E. with Goodlad, D. *Backstairs Life in a Country House* (Newton Abbot, 1982)

Barnardo's, Dr, *Annual Reports of Homes*

Beddoe, D. *Back to Home and Duty, Women between the Wars, 1918-1939* (London, 1989)

Bedford, John, Duke of, *A Silver-plated Spoon* (London, 1959 edn)

Berghahn, M. *German-Jewish Refugees in England* (New York, 1984)

Braybon, G. *Women Workers in the First World War* (London, 1981)

Briar, C. *Working for Women? Gendered Work and Welfare Policies in Twentieth-Century Britain* (London, 1997)

Brittney, L. *The Which? Guide to Domestic Help* (London, 1998)

Burnett, J. (ed.), *Useful Toil* (London, 1974)

Butler, C.V. *Domestic Service. An Enquiry by the Women's Industrial Council* (London, 1916)

Byrne, D. (ed.), *Waiting for Change?* (Low Pay Pamphlet No. 42, London, July 1986)

Carrothers, W.A. *Emigration from the British Isles* (London, 1965 edn)

Chorley, K. *Manchester Made Them* (London, 1950)

Community Action, No. 67 (London, November 1984)

Contarini, P. *The Savoy was my Oyster* (London, 1976)

Contract Clean-up. An Outline of Trends and Conditions in the Contract Cleaning Industry (Greater London Council Economic Policy Group Strategy document no. 9, 1983)

Cox, R. 'The Role of Ethnicity in Shaping the Domestic Employment Sector in Britain' in Janet Henshall Momsen (ed.), *Gender, Migration and Domestic Service* (London and New York, 1999)

Cox, R. 'Exploring the Growth of Paid Domestic Labour: a case study of London', forthcoming in *Geography*.

Dallington, S. *Around Foxton, Memories of an Edwardian*

Childhood (Wymeswold, 1991)

Darcy, G.H. *Problems and Changes in Women's Work in England and Wales, 1918-1939* (London University Ph.D. thesis, 1984)

Davison, I. *Etiquette for Women. A Book of Modern Manners and Customs* (London, 1928)

Dawes, F. *Not in Front of the Servants. Domestic Service in England 1850-1939* (London, 1973)

—, 'The Dying Reign of the Pantry', *Daily Telegraph Magazine*, 6 July, 1972.

Devonshire, Duchess of, *The Estate. A View from Chatsworth* (London, 1990)

—, *The House. A Portrait of Chatsworth* (London, 1982)

Dickens, M. *One Pair of Hands* (Harmondsworth, 1972 edn)

Eley, G. *And Here is Mr Streeter* (London, 1950)

Elliott, D.M. *The Status of Domestic Work in the United Kingdom with Special Reference to the National Institute of Houseworkers* (Geneva, 1951)

Ellis, J. (ed.), *Thatched with Gold. The Memoirs of Mabell, Countess of Airlie* (London, 1962)

Festing, S. *Gertrude Jekyll* (London, 1993 edn)

Field, L. *Bendor. The Golden Duke of Westminster* (London, 1986 edn)

Firth, V. *The Psychology of the Servant Problem* (London, 1925)

Foley, W. *The Forest Trilogy* (Oxford, 1992 edn)

Foyster, J. & Proud, K. *Gamekeeper* (Newton Abbot, 1986)

Gathorne Hardy, J. *The Rise and Fall of the British Nanny* (London, 1972)

'Gibbs, M.A.', *The Year of the Nannies* (London, 1960)

Girls' Friendly Society, Annual Reports of the

Göpfert, R. (ed.), *Ich kam allein. Die Rettung von zehntausend jüdischen Kindern nach England 1938-39* (München, 1997 edn)

Gordon, E. & Breitenbach, E. (ed.), *The World is Ill Divided. Women's Work in Scotland in the Nineteenth and Early Twentieth Centuries* (Edinburgh, 1990)

Goring, O.G. *50 Years of Service* (London, 1960)

Gorst, F.J. *Of Carriages and Kings* (London, 1956)

Gregory, B. *A Gardener's Life. Memories of Gardening on some of the Great English Private Estates* (privately printed n.d. [*c.* 1999])

Gregson, N. and Lowe, M. *Servicing the Middle Classes. Class, Gender and Waged Domestic Labour in Contemporary Britain* (London and New York, 1994)

Haggard, L.R. *I Walked by Night* by *The King of the Norfolk Poachers* (Ipswich, 1974 edn)

Hall, E. *Canary Girls and Stockpots* (Luton, 1977)

Harrison, B. 'For Church, Queen and Family: The Girls' Friendly Society', *Past and Present*, No. 61 (1973)

Harrison, M. 'Domestic Service Between the Wars: The Experiences of Two Rural Women', *Oral History*, Vol.

16, No.1 (spring, 1988)

Harrison, R. (ed.), *Gentlemen's Gentlemen. My Friends in Service* (London, 1978 edn)

Harrison, R. *Rose: My Life in Service* (London, 1975)

Heath-Stubbs, M. *Friendship's Highway* (London, 1935)

Hirschfield, G. (ed.), *Exile in Great Britain. Refugees from Hitler's Germany* (Leamington Spa, 1984)

Horn, P. 'Hunting the servants: The role of servant training centres between the wars', *Genealogists' Magazine*, Vol. 26, No.8 (December 1999)

—, *Ladies of the Manor* (Stroud, 1997 edn)

—, *Rural Life in England in the First World War* (Dublin, 1984)

—, *The Rise and Fall of the Victorian Servant* (Stroud, 1995 edn)

—, 'Training and Status in Domestic Service: The Role of the League of Skilled Housecraft, 1922-1942', *History of Education Society Bulletin*, No. 65 (May 2000)

—, *Women in the 1920s* (Stroud, 1995)

Horne, E. *More Winks* (London, 1932)

—, *What the Butler Winked At* (London, 1923)

Humphries, S. and Hopwood, B. *Green and Pleasant Land. The Untold Story of Country Life in Twentieth Century Britain* (London, 1999)

Humphris, T. *Garden Glory* (London, 1970)

Hunt, A. and Fox, J. *The Home Help Service in England and Wales*, SS.407 (London, 1970)

Inch, A.R. *Reminiscences of a Life in Private Service* (London, 1999)

Jackson, A.A. *Semi-Detached London. Suburban Development, Life and Transport, 1900-39* (Didcot, 1991 edn)

Jackson, Maj. Gen. Sir L.C. *History of the United Service Club* (London, 1937)

Jackson, S. *The Savoy. The Romance of a Great Hotel* (London, 1964)

Johnson, S.C. *Emigration from the United Kingdom to North America 1763-1912* (London, 1966 edn)

Jones, D.C. (ed.), *The Social Survey of Merseyside,* Vol. II (Liverpool and London, 1934)

Jones, H. (ed.), *Duty and Citizenship. The Correspondence and Papers of Violet Markham, 1896-1953* (London, 1994)

Jones, K. and Hewitt, T. *A.H. Jones of Grosvenor House* (London, 1971)

Jones, T. *A Diary with Letters 1931-1950* (London, 1954)

Josephs, Z. *Survivors. Jewish Refugees in Birmingham 1933-1945* (Warley, 1988)

Khan, S. and Kirkham, S. *Behind the Painted Smiles. A Report on Pay and Conditions in the Hotel and Catering Sector* (Greater Manchester Low Pay Unit, 1995)

King, E. *The Green Baize Door* (Bath, 1974 edn)

Kushner, T. 'An Alien Occupation - Jewish Refugees and

Domestic Service in Britain, 1933-1948' in Werner E. Mosse et al. (ed.), *Second Chance. Two Centuries of German-speaking Jews in the United Kingdom* (Tübingen, 1991)

—, 'Asylum or Servitude? Refugee domestics in Britain, 1933-1945', *Bulletin of the Society for the Study of Labour History*. Vol. 53, Pt. 3 (1988)

—, 'Politics and Race, Gender and Class: Refugees, Fascists and Domestic Service in Britain, 1933-1940' in Tony Kushner and Kenneth Lunn (ed.), *The Politics of Marginality. Race, the Radical Right and Minorities in Twentieth Century Britain* (London, 1990)

Lafitte, F. *The Internment of Aliens* (Harmondsworth, 1940)

Laurie, K. *Cricketer Preferred. Estate Workers at Lyme Park 1898-1946* (Lyme Park Joint Committee, n.d. [*c.* 1981])

Lee, D. *Great Estates* (London, 2000)

Lewenhak, S. *Women and Trade Unions* (London, 1977)

Lewis, L. *The Private Life of a Country House 1912-39* (London, 1982 edn)

Lewis, R. and Maude, A. *The English Middle Classes* (London, 1953 ed)

Lipman, M. *How Was It For You?* (Oxford, 1989 edn)

Macmillan, H. *Winds of Change 1914-1919* (London, 1966)

Markham, V. *Return Passage* (London, 1953)

Marsh, D.C. *The Changing Social Structure of England and Wales, 1871-1961* (London, 1965)

Marwick, A. *The Deluge. British Society and the First World War* (London, 1965)

Matheson, J. and Summerfield, C. (ed.), *Social Focus on Older People* (London, 1999)

Men Without Work. A Report made to the Pilgrim Trust (Cambridge, 1938)

Middleton, N. *When Family Failed. The Treatment of Children in the Care of the Community during the First Half of the Twentieth Century* (London, 1971)

Mistress and Maid (anonymous pamphlet issued by the Domestic Bureau, London, April 1940)

Morgan, J. and Richards, A. *A Paradise out of a Common Field. The Pleasures and Plenty of the Victorian Garden* (New York, 1990)

Mosse, W. et al. (ed.), *Second Chance. Two Centuries of German-speaking Jews in the United Kingdom* (Tübingen, 1991)

Mrs Beeton's Household Management (London, 1923 edn and London, 1949 edn)

Mullins, S. and Griffiths, G. *Cap and Apron. An Oral History of Domestic Service in the Shires, 1880-1950* (Leicestershire Museums, Art Galleries and Records Series: The Harborough Series, No.2, 1986)

Mursell, N. *Come Dawn, Come Dusk. Fifty Years a Gamekeeper for the Dukes of Westminster* (Cambridge, 1996 edn)

—, *Green and Pleasant Land. A Countryman Remembers* (London, 1983)

Annual Reports of National Institute of Houseworkers

Annual Report of the National Vigilance Association for 1934-35 (1935)

Noakes, D. *The Town Beehive. A Young Girl's Lot. Brighton 1910-1934* (Brighton, 1995 edn)

Noel, D. *Five to Seven. The Story of a 1920s Childhood* (London, 1978)

Nowell-Smith, S. (ed.), *Edwardian England 1901-1914* (London, 1964)

Nudds, A. *The Woods Belong to Me* (Cambridge, 1998 edn)

Parr, J. *Labouring Children* (London, 1980)

Partridge, F. *A Pacifist's War* (London, 1978)

Patterson, S. *Dark Strangers. A Sociological Study of the Absorption of a recent West Indian migrant group in Brixton, south London* (London, 1963)

People's Autobiography of Hackney. Working Lives, Vol. II, *1945-77* (London, 1977)

Phizacklea, A. (ed.), *One way Ticket. Migration and Female Labour* (London, 1983)

Powell, M. *Below Stairs* (London, 1970 edn.)

Pugh, M. *Women and the Women's Movement in Britain 1914-1959* (Basingstoke, 1992)

Pullinger, J. and Summerfield, C. (ed.), *Social Focus on Women and Men* (London, 1998)

Rennie, J. *Every Other Sunday. The Autobiography of a*

Kitchenmaid (London, 1955)

Roberts, E. *Women and Families. An Oral History 1940-1970* (Oxford, 1995)

Robinson, D. *Memories of Upper Bangor in the 20s and 30s* (Bangor, n.d. [*c.* 1999])

Robinson, J.M. *The Country House at War* (London, 1989)

Rose, J. *For the Sake of the Children. Inside Dr Barnardo's: 130 Years of Caring for Children* (London, 1987)

Rose, L. *The Erosion of Childhood. Child Oppression in Britain 1860-1918* (London and New York, 1991)

Rowntree, B.S. *Poverty. A Study of Town Life* (London, 1903 edn)

Russell, P. *Butler Royal* (London, 1982)

Rutter, J. *The Young Women's Christian Association of Great Britain 1900-1925. An Organisation of Change* (University of Warwick MA thesis, 1986)

Sambrook, P.A. *The Country House Servant* (Stroud, 1999)

—, *A Servants' Place. An Account of the Servants at Shugborough* (Staffordshire County Museum: Shugborough Estate, 1989)

Schneider, B. *Exile. A Memoir of 1939.* Erika Bourguignon and Barbara Hill Rigney (eds) (Columbus, Ohio, 1998)

Segal, L. *Other People's Homes* (London, 1965)

Llewellyn Smith, Sir H. (ed.), *The New Survey of London Life and Labour*, Vol. II (London, 1931) and Vol. VIII

(London, 1934)

Statutory and Agreement-Based Provisions on Certain Aspects of the Organisation of Working Time in the Cleaning Industry. European Social Dialogue: Document Series (Brussels, 1993)

Stokes, P. *Norland 1892-1992* (Hungerford, 1992)

Strachey, R. *The Cause* (London, 1978 edn)

Streatfeild, N. (ed.), *The Day Before Yesterday* (London, 1956)

Stroud, J. *Thirteen Penny Stamps. The Story of the Church of England Children's Society (Waifs and Strays) from 1881 to the 1970s* (London, 1971)

Summerfield, P. *Reconstructing Women's Wartime Lives* (Manchester, 1998)

—, *Women Workers in the Second World War. Production and Patriarchy in Conflict* (London, 1984)

Swaisland, C. *Servants and Gentlewomen to the Golden Land. The Emigration of Single Women from Britain to Southern Africa 1820-1939* (Oxford and Pietermaritzburg, S. Africa, 1993)

Sykes, C. *Nancy. The Life of Lady Astor* (London, 1979 edn)

Taken to the Cleaners: The Lincolnshire Experience (SCAT for East Midlands NUPE/NALGO, November, 1988)

Taylor, P. 'Daughters and mothers - maids and mistresses: domestic service between the wars' in John Clarke, Charles Critcher and Richard Johnson ed., *Working*

Class Culture. Studies in History and Theory (London, 1979)

Thomas, A. *Wait and See* (London, 1944)

Thoms, D. *War, Industry and Society. The Midlands 1939-45* (London and New York, 1989)

Tillyard, Sir F. *Unemployment Insurance in Great Britain 1911-1948* (Leigh on Sea, 1949)

Annual Reports of the Trades Union Congress, for 1924, 1932, 1938 and 1939

Troubridge, Lady. *The Book of Etiquette* (London, 1931 edn)

Turner, E.S. *What the Butler Saw. Two Hundred and Fifty Years of the Servant Problem* (London, 1962)

Turner, T.W. *Memoirs of a Gamekeeper (Elveden, 1868-1953)* (London, 1954)

Tyack, G. 'Service on the Cliveden Estate Between the Wars', *Oral History*, Vol. 5, No.1 (spring 1977)

Walton, J.K. *The Blackpool Landlady. A Social History* (Manchester, 1978)

Waterson, M. (ed.), *The Country House Remembered. Recollections of Life Between the Wars* (London, 1985)

—, *The Servants' Hall. A Domestic History of Erddig* (London, 1980)

Waugh, E. *Put Out More Flags* (Harmondsworth, 1972 edn)

Duchess of Westrninster, L. *Grace and Favour* (London, 1961)

Willes, M. *Country House Estates* (London, 1996)

Winstanley, M. *Life in Kent at the Turn of the Century* (Folkestone, 1978)

Woollacott, A. *On Her their Lives Depend. Munitions Workers in the Great War* (Berkeley, California, 1994)

INTERNET WEB SITES

Federation of Employment and Recruitment Agencies, www.fres.co.uk

Ivor Spencer's School for Butler Administrators/Personal Assistants, www.ivorspencer.com/butler.htm

ACKNOWLEDGEMENTS

Ishould like to thank all who have helped with the preparation of this book, either by providing photographs and documents or in other ways. I am especially grateful to the many people who responded so generously to my appeals for reminiscences of domestic servant life in the twentieth century; their contributions are acknowledged in the notes. However, I should particularly like to thank Arthur R. Inch, Mrs Mary Cocking and Mrs Sheila Whiting for their patience in responding to my many queries. Anne Jüssen of the Frauen Museum, Bonn, also devoted much time to transcribing the fascinating and lengthy correspondence between herself and her friend, Adele, in 1969-70, when Adele was an *au pair* in England.

Others have given permission for the use of documents and photographs and to them also my thanks are due. They include Mrs Anne Monk of the Girls' Friendly Society, David Ball of *myhome*, John Kirkham of

Barnardo's Photographic Archive, Jim Garretts, Director of Manchester Jewish Museum, David J. Brazier of Studley College Trust, William Weber of Mrs Hunt's Agency, London, the Guardian and Observer Syndication, and Rosie Cox of Coventry University, who provided details of her own researches into modern domestic service in London. Miss Eileen R. Hawkins kindly gave permission for the use of the Young Women's Christian Association records kept at the Modern Records Centre at the University of Warwick. Stirling Smith Art Gallery provided photocopies of servant reminiscences in their possession.

I have received much efficient help and guidance from staff in the libraries, record offices, museums and university archives where I have worked and to them, too, I should like to express my gratitude. They include the Archival Resource Centre, University of Essex; the Bodleian Library, Oxford; the British Library; the British Library Newspaper Library, Colindale; the British Library of Political and Economic Science, London School of Economics; Cardiff Local History Library; the Women's Library at the London Metropolitan University; the Imperial War Museum Photograph and Sound Archives; Leicestershire Record Office; the London Metropolitan Archives; Maidenhead Reference Library; Margate Local History Library; Market Harborough Museum; the Modern Records Centre, University of Warwick; the National Archives, Kew; the Rural History Centre,

University of Reading; Staffordshire County Council Arts and Museum Service, especially Helen Ruthven at Shugborough; the TUC Library at the London Metropolitan University and its librarian, Christine Coates; the University of Reading Archives and the former archivist, Michael Bott; and the Wiener Library, London, and its head librarian, Colin Clarke.

Finally, as always, I owe a great debt to my late husband for his unfailing help and advice, and for his company on many research 'expeditions'. Without him this book could not have been written.

PAMELA HORN, April 2001 and 2012

Also available from Amberley Publishing

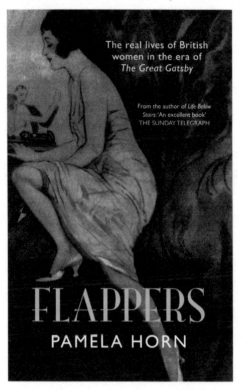

The real lives of British women in the era of The Great Gatsby

For many women the 1920s was a time of change after the pressures – and opportunities – of the First World War. For a number, war casualties meant a life of spinsterhood, which some turned to good account by enjoying their new independence.

Drawing on family papers, contemporary publications and archive research, complemented by a wealth of photographs, cartoons and other illustrations, this book examines how women responded to the new challenges and difficulties of those years, from the revival of the round of high society by the social elite, to the lives of the new middle-class professionals, and working-class women employed in the still-traditional milieu of factory and domestic services.

£9.99 Paperback
40 photographs
256 pages
978-1-4456-1402-1

Available from from all good bookshops or to order direct
Please call **01453-847-800**
www.amberleybooks.com

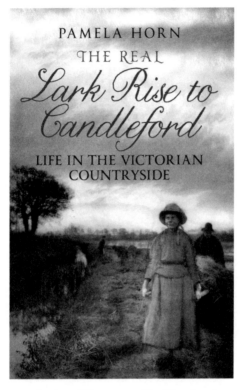

Also available from Amberley Publishing

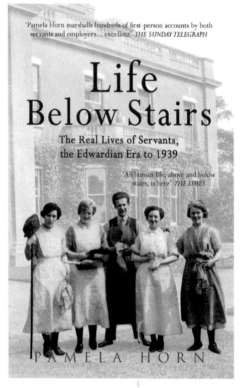

'Pamela Horn marshalls hundreds of first-person accounts by both servants and employers... excellent' *THE SUNDAY TELEGRAPH*

Life Below Stairs

The Real Lives of Servants, the Edwardian Era to 1939

'All human life, above and below stairs, is here' *THE TIMES*

P A M E L A   H O R N

'Pamela Horn marshals hundreds of first-person accounts by both servant and employers... an excellent book' THE SUNDAY TELEGRAPH

By the end of the 1920s domestic service remained the largest female occupation in Britain. We view it today as an undesirable job, owing to the class divide it has come to represent, and this is reflected in the portrayals of mistresses and servants in books and on the screen in such dramas as *Upstairs Downstairs* and *Downton Abbey*. But what do we really know about how girls felt when taking up these positions in other people's houses, or how they were treated? Pamela Horn uses first-hand accounts and reminiscences, as well as official records and newspaper reports, to extract the truth about the lives and status of men and women in domestic service from 1900 to 1939.

£9.99 Paperback
40 photographs
192 pages
978-1-4456-1008-5

Available from all good bookshops or to order direct
Please call **01453-847-800**
www.amberleybooks.com